THE AMERICAN
Jeep

THE AMERICAN
Jeep
In War and Peace

KURT WILLINGER AND GENE GURNEY

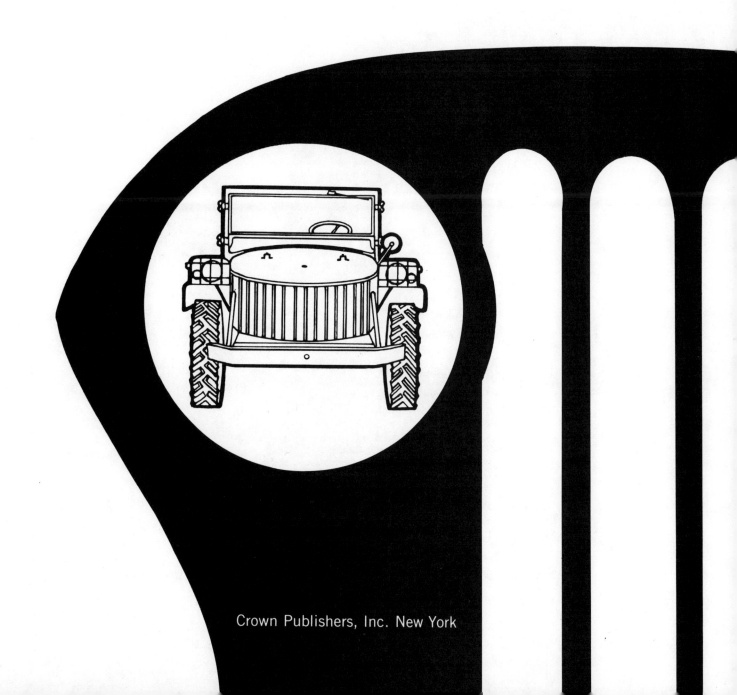

Crown Publishers, Inc. New York

Published by Crown Publishers, Inc., One Park Avenue, New York, New
York 10016, and simultaneously in Canada by General Publishing
Company Limited

Manufactured in the United States of America

Library of Congress Cataloging in Publication Data
Willinger, Kurt.
The American Jeep in war and peace.
Includes index.
1. Jeep automobile.   I. Gurney, Gene.
II. Title.
TL215.J44W53   1983   355.8'3   82-13974
ISBN: 0-517-54734-1 (cloth)
ISBN: 0-517-54735-X (paper)

10 9 8 7 6 5 4 3 2 1
First Edition

Dedicated to my Dad who taught me the joy
of feeling useful. And to my partner, Gene,
who as always did most of the work.

Contents

Acknowledgments

Cover design and graphics throughout: Warren Rogers

Original art on jacket/cover: John Ball, Frank Wagner, Skidmore Sahratian Studio, Troy, Michigan

Researchers: Jeannie Savino; Doris Kahn; Bill Williams; Ernest Kahn, T Sgt. U.S. Army (ret.); Gene Richmond, American Motors; Jeff Wright, American Motors General.

Technical assistance: Eileen Maxwell, Hawkeye Surplus

Department of Defense: Bettie Sprigg, chief of the magazine and book branch

Defense Audio Visual Agency: Vicki Destefano, chief of the reference library

Preface

In A.D. 398 the Goths challenged the mighty legions of the Roman Empire . . . and won. The barbarian general Alaric accomplished this unheard-of feat with a highly mobile cavalry: expert horsemen who with speed and surprise routed Rome's mighty legions. Rome sent its most experienced commander, Gerantius, to crush the barbarian army, but in spite of superior forces, the legions were cut to ribbons by the unconventional mobility of the Goths.

First Greece fell to the barbarians and then, with the conquest of Italy, the rest of the Roman Empire. Warfare would never be the same. For now, the use of a highly mobile fighting force had become a primary military tactic.

The jeep came into being as one more refinement in the tactic of mobility.

Foreword

by William C. Westmoreland
General, U.S. Army (Ret.)

Battlefield mobility is vital to the success of any military operation. It takes reliable, sturdy vehicles to withstand the rigors of modern warfare. In Vietnam this requirement was being severely tested —under the most trying conditions: an often primitive road system, monsoon rains, heavy jungle, and the constant need for high mobility down to the squad level.

Tested and proved in World War II and the Korean Conflict, the jeep did not need any introduction when the Vietnam War started. Here, under the most tortuous of conditions it provided our troops with much of the flexibility to move about, thus earning the respect of our adversaries whether the fighting was in the hills, the hamlets, or in the countryside. As far as the American soldier in Vietnam was concerned, the jeep continued to be a legend in the annals of modern warfare.

Introduction

This book presents a view of American history and social change through the evolution of a single tenacious mechanical entity: the 1/4-ton reconnaissance vehicle known as the jeep.

The jeep was originally designed for war and performed beyond all expectations. As time and needs changed, so did the jeep, evolving, adjusting, and improving to become the vehicle it is today. Yet one thing has stayed the same. The very first GI who drove it, knew it. Anyone at the wheel of a modern jeep will feel it. And that is the "can do" spirit, which communicates swiftly and profoundly that this small machine will never let you down.

That spirit is what this book is all about.

THE AMERICAN Jeep

IN THE BEGINNING . . .

In the early part of 1980 two polls were taken, one in the United States and the other in Japan, that showed the jeep to be the "most popular" and "the most memorable" motor vehicle in the world. The results of these two surveys came as no surprise to the owners of the 3 million jeeps of various models built by the American Motors Company and its predecessor companies, Willys-Overland and Kaiser. Nor did the results surprise the many millions of GIs who over the years drove, and are still driving, the military jeeps—the Willys and Ford jeeps of World War II and then the M-38 and the M-151 models. GIs returned to civilian life and countless numbers of them—along with their civilian counterparts—bought in unprecedented numbers the commercial and private ver-

In 1937 the U.S. Army, in its search for a low-silhouette, lightweight vehicle, built a demonstration model of what they were looking for in this type of vehicle. The demonstration model, officially known as the Howie-Wiley Carrier, was called the Belly Flopper by all who rode it. But it turned out to be the basic model for the automobile industry to add to and change until they came up with a vehicle that would meet the army's needs—the jeep. Col. Robert G. Howie and M/Sgt. Melvin C. Wiley were the two army personnel who developed the model.

Delmar Roos, chief engineer of Willys-Overland in Toledo, Ohio, had been championing a lighter automobile design for years. He spent many late hours at his desk working out the details for such a vehicle, but came to the conclusion that the Belly Flopper had too low a level of gravity and that the 1,300-pound limit the army was seeking in basic weight was also too low. However, Willys decided to submit a bid and build a model. It turned out to weigh 2,423 pounds.

Engineer Roos triumphed with his decision to win the army over to a higher center of gravity and a heavier vehicle. The army won, too, with a vehicle that two presidents of the United States termed the "most important contribution" and the "most valuable weapon" of World War II. In this photograph taken in 1943 at Fort Benning, Georgia, the highly successful Roos-designed jeep and the Belly Flopper of 1937 stand side by side.

Ward M. Canaday, chairman of the board of Willys-Overland, started discussions with the U.S. Army in 1939 to help them realize their requirement for a low-silhouette military vehicle in case the United States should become embroiled in the European war. Three years later, the chairman drove the 100,000th jeep off the assembly line.

sions of this vehicle that they so admired and respected.

Over the years the term *jeep* has become a generic expression. In Japan, the people refer to Toyota and Suburu 4-wheel drives as jeeps. Throughout Britain and the rest of Europe, similarly designed vehicles are also called jeeps. In America, the same is true; more people call the other manufactured 4-wheel-drive vehicles "jeep" than Broncos or whatever their name may be.

Regardless of the worldwide imitations of the original World War II American jeep, only the official generations of successors by Kaiser, Ford, and American Motors have retained the ruggedness and reliability of the original and the broad range of appeal to satisfy so many different needs and tastes. Although the jeep is not a fashionable-looking vehicle in its basic form, American Motors has introduced it in a popular luxury line, as well as some very exciting "macho" models.

Of all the motor vehicles manufactured in the history of the automobile, only the jeep has retained its basic design. The Volkswagen "Beetle" was coming close to the record, but the company gave up in 1977 and materially changed its design.

Today, in a military pool, one can see an early-model jeep parked alongside a model that is thirty-five years older and another that is three generations younger, and it will be difficult to see much difference between them.

In tracing the history of the jeep, we must go back to the late 1930s when the U.S. Army was looking for a small, general-purpose vehicle that would serve as an armored personnel carrier for three people. The army wanted something that would serve equally well as a utility vehicle in peacetime and as part of its weaponry arsenal in wartime. It had to have 4-wheel drive for versatility in different terrains, and it must be light enough to qualify as a 1/4-ton carrier. Responding to the army's needs, the automobile industry developed a number of experimental vehicles of this kind.

According to which top automotive engineers of that early period you talk to, the basic design of the jeep came from one of three vehicles: the 1936 Ford Marmon Herrington 1/2-ton 4 × 4 (4-wheel drive), or the Minneapolis-Moline 4 × 4 military tractor of 1939, or the Dodge 1/2-ton 4 × 4 command reconnaissance truck of 1940. The latter two were actually called jeeps—from the designation GPs (General-Purpose vehicles).

There is little disagreement among the design engineers, however, that the general body design for the first jeeps originated with the American Bantam Company entry in the government's first pre-World War II competition (1940) for a rugged 1/4-ton, 4 × 4 general-purpose truck. The term 1/4 ton here refers to a motor vehicle that could effectively carry a load of 1/4 ton (500 pounds) plus 100 percent—that is, 1,000 pounds.

The experts also agree that the Ford entry in the competition brought forth the tough front-end-suspension systems and the design of the rear body that worked their way into the final contract awarded to Willys-Overland Motors of Toledo, Ohio, where all the best features of the three competitors were standardized into one vehicle.

The 4-cyclinder engine developed by Willys' chief engineer, Delmar Roos, performed so well in all of the tests that it won the contract for the mass production of 16,000 of the 1/4-ton 4 × 4s for

the company. (The procurement officer of the Quartermaster Corps confided to the competitors at the time of the contract letting in July 1941 that the Willys-Overland entry was also the lowest bidder.) The initial order for 16,000 units to Willys was then extended to 18,600 and the army, fearing that their one source (Willys) might be sabotaged, approached the Ford Motor Company to be a second source. Ford agreed and started to manufacture the vehicles also.

But we are jumping ahead of our story. The U.S. Army's original specifications included a limiting total-empty-weight requirement of 1,308 pounds. To satisfy this and the army's other requirements would require an engineering miracle. The call for proposals was answered by the Bantam, Ford, and Willys-Overland companies. The three submitted vehicle models in 1940 for initial testing at Fort Myer in Arlington, Virginia, and for final tests at Holabird Army Depot in Baltimore, Maryland. Each company's models performed so well that the Quartermaster Corps awarded contracts to all three for 1,500 additional vehicles each for "a final field testing" before the big contract would be let. The testing was to take place at various sites throughout the United States, Alaska, and the Hawaiian Islands during the winter of 1940/41.

Since a 1,308-pound vehicle was not practical in this case, the army changed its procurement specification to 2,160 pounds. Bantam was already under that figure with a 2,030-pound entry. Ford and the eventual winner, Willys, had to rush home from the Holabird testing and drastically cut down on the weight of their vehicles. Willys was able to lower the weight of 2,423 pounds for its Quad (as they called their vehicle at that time) to

2,154, including a reduction to only one coat of paint. "The application of another coat," explained chief engineer Roos, "would have put us over the limit."

Willys designated its 1,500 test vehicles the MA model. After the testing, most of these vehicles were given to the Soviet Union under the Lend-Lease Act. If a reader should ever happen somehow to locate one of these jeeps, it can be checked against the serial numbers, which went from W-2018932 to W-2020431.

After winning the second phase of the competition and the big contract, Willys started its production of the standardized jeep and designated it the MB model, with serial numbers that started at MB100,000.

Ford had gone back to Detroit from Holabird and changed its Pygmy into a 2,160-pound vehicle that was then called the Ford GP, but these efforts were to no avail—for Willys won the contract. Most of the Ford GPs, after testing, were sent to Great Britain on lend-lease, as were the Bantams. Although losing the "Battle of the Jeep" to Willys, Ford as runner-up did produce an additional 2,150 GPs under the 1942 Quartermaster contract. But they were required to install an improved engine over the one used in the competition—a Ford Ferguson "Dearborn" tractor engine. This was another modified tractor engine, still 4 cyclinders— a model NNA, 119.5 C10, 45 bhp rated at 3,600 rpm. Ford also continued to manufacture jeeps from 1942 to 1945, as did Willys; however, the Ford jeep was a GP-W, a General Purpose-Willys, made under a license from Willys.

Bantam, for the final competition, developed and produced in the required numbers a model 40 BRC engine (a Continental

4-cylinder with 45 bhp), which, while more powerful, nevertheless lost out to the Willys engine. Although the Bantam vehicle was well designed and manufactured, it was excluded from mass production under the Willys license because Bantam did not have sufficient facilities in their Butler, Pennsylvania, plant to build the jeep in the large numbers that the army needed.

After Willys won the contract award, the army met at Holabird with the Willys executives and asked that the 16,000 models to be produced contain the following fourteen major changes or alterations in the final standard design:

1. An improved air cleaner in the carburetor.
2. A larger, 6-volt generator having 40-ampere capacity, which would be the standard of other army trucks.
3. A 15-gallon gasoline tank (compared to the 10- or 11-gallon tanks in the three test models).
4. A 5-inch sealed-beam headlight with a double-filament bulb that had been developed by the army automotive engineers.
5. A 2-H-type, 6-volt, standardized army battery in place of the passenger-car batteries used on the three test models.
6. The hand brake to be located in the center of the vehicle so it could be operated by either the driver or a passenger.
7. Relocating of the remote-control gearshift to the center of the floor of the vehicle as it was in most other government vehicles.
8. Setting the steering tie rods higher up from the axle to protect them against injury from road conditions.
9. Better protection for the hydraulic brake hose.
10. A double-bow canvas top (rather than a one-bow top) for greater headroom for the driver.
11. An axe and shovel to be installed on the outside of the vehicle.
12. Spring shackles to provide seals to keep water and dirt out and hold in the lubricants.
13. Blackout lights as they existed in other government vehicles.
14. Power takeoff—an employment of engineering for a faster first-gear acceleration of the vehicle.

While the vehicles were in production, both the army and the companies introduced further engineering changes, such as "combat wheels," in which the ordinary drop-center wheel was given a split rim that would permit a vehicle with a flat tire to travel a longer distance.

The end product of the changes introduced by the army and the companies was a vehicle embodying more automotive-engineering innovations than any other in automotive history up to that time— and probably since. These numerous innovations are undoubtedly responsible for the jeep being the versatile vehicle it is today.

When Pearl Harbor brought the United States into the war on December 7, 1941, the armed forces were to benefit in many ways from the early and wise development of the jeep.

The first Willys entry in the 1940 competition had a rounded front hood and grille similar to the American Bantam Car Company entry. This copy was called the Quad by both the Willys Company and the U.S. Army personnel who tested it. (Note that "Quad" is stenciled on the bumper.)

The Willys candidate in the competition was driven to the Holabird Army Depot in Baltimore, Maryland, by Irving "Red" Hausmann, a Willys-Overland test driver, who then drove it to Washington, D.C., for a demonstration of its 4-wheel prowess on the steps of the Capitol.

Many people of World War II vintage erroneously believe that the name "jeep" derives from E. C. Segar's cartoon strip "Popeye," where a character called Eugene the Jeep appeared from April 1937 onward. But long after Eugene disappeared, the vehicle in question was still being called the Quad, the Peep, and G.P. (General Purpose). Army personnel of that period, as well as the employees at Willys at the time (including the authors), have concluded that the "GP" name used in the army and at Ford became "jeep."

The three competing vehicles were all good enough for the U.S. Army to grant their companies a contract for 1,500 more of each for further competition in "worldwide operations." But Willys-Overland was told to slim their model down in weight before mass-producing. Engineer Roos solved the problem of his company's jeep being in excess (263 pounds) of army specifications by cutting it to the bone, "including even spreading the paint thin." Testing in Toledo showed the effect of the lighter-weight jeep on gravity.

A Bantam model being used in a combat exercise in April 1940 at the Infantry School at Fort Benning. The soldiers there called it the Peep. This model is equipped with a mortar piece installed on the rear seat. The army serial numbers for the 1,500 Bantams were W-2015919–W-2017268. Even though the Bantam lost the final competition, the army awarded a contract to them for an additional 1,000 copies for lend-lease to Great Britain and Russia. These were produced before Pearl Harbor day, December 7, 1941.

The Willys model that went into production on the contract for 1,500 copies was designated MA and carried the army serial numbers W-2018932 through W-2020431. After the testing was completed and Willys won the competition on its low bid, most of the 1,500 copies were sent to Russia. At this point, Willys changed the vehicle's front end to the box-shaped hood and grille more resembling the Ford General Purpose model, and also adopted the name "jeep," from the phonics of "GP."

Below: the 4,500 original test models were shipped to army units all over the United States, Alaska, and Hawaii for operational testing and service. A Willys is put through a grueling trial run in the desert of Death Valley.

Royal Canadian Ordnance Corps officers in July 1941 put the Willys through its paces in a mudhole on the test course at Holabird Depot in Maryland.

The American Bantam entry in the final competition, 1941.

Soldiers demonstrating the Ford "jeep" at Fort Sam Houston, Texas, during a press conference in March 1941. The Ford serial numbers were 2017418–2018931. The key in the demonstrations and tests was to take the hurdles and make a four-point landing.

The Bantam being tested for durability in snow at Camp Globe, Wisconsin, in 1941. Note the chains on the tires.

Jeeps being tested up hills at Fort Sam Houston, Texas, in 1941.

In May 1942 at Fort Ord, California, a jeep passes the familiar steed of the 107th Cavalry Regiment, one of the first units to convert from horse mounts to mechanized vehicles.

Above: Within thirty days of conversion to mechanization, a troop from the 107th Cavalry Regiment consisting of a scout car and three jeeps sets up an effective ambush maneuver at a crossroad. This training exercise was to be repeated countless times in combat in World War II, with results that never would have been possible with horses.

Right: Four West Point cadets on summer duty at Fort Benning, Georgia, testing both the jeep and the new army helmets that were to replace the World War I ones.

By 1942 all kinds of armament were being added to the jeeps at Fort Benning to ready them for combat.

The Benning trainees were equipped with goggles for protection from the dust that was raised by the jeeps on the training course.

At Camp Gruber, Oklahoma, the spare tire was moved across the inside front of the jeep in an experiment to allow for faster access.

First-echelon maintenance had to be established for drivers of jeeps so that they could lift the hood and check the basic moving parts for proper function to prevent a future breakdown. Such preventive maintenance was advocated at Fort Oglethorpe in Georgia.

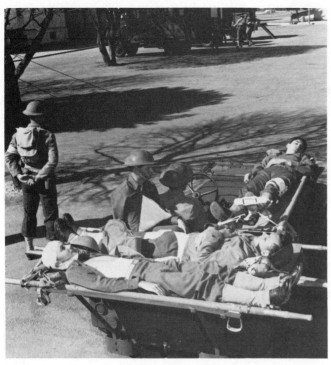

Soldiers at Fort Sam Houston, Texas, testing ambulance jeeps in an exercise simulating combat.

At Fort Benning, Georgia, training was expanded with instruction in driving a jeep into a mock-up scale model of an airplane (C-46).

Soldiers of the 105th Medical Battalion, Fort Jackson, South Carolina, tow a waterproofed canvas-wrapped jeep across a stream in July 1942.

An army corporal changes his mind about crossing a stream and backs up. Fort Oglethorpe, Georgia, August 1942.

At Fort Funston, Kansas, in 1942, the 9th Engineers built practice bridges for the 2nd Cavalry Division's jeeps to cross rivers.

An experimental jeep trailer was developed by the 1st Cavalry Brigade at Fort Bliss, Texas, in the fall of 1941.

Despite the army's efforts to keep the weight of this 1/4-ton government truck at 1,300 pounds, the final MB model off the production line weighed 2,554 pounds. Although there were many versions of the MB built during the war, it was the standard vehicle. The first standard MB model weighed 2,450 pounds and was 2 inches longer than the MA. The first of the Willys MB models appeared in 1941.

Jeeps soon became a preferred means of giving general officers highly mobile command transportation. A Ford (*left*) and a Bantam (*right*) at New River, North Carolina, during 1st Division practice landing operations.

General officers soon adopted the practice of driving the jeeps themselves. Maj. Gen. Robert L. Eichelberger, newly named (March 1942) commanding general of the 77th Infantry Division at Fort Jackson, South Carolina, drives a jeep staff vehicle with his aide as passenger, on their way to an inspection of the camp.

By mid-1942 enough jeeps were rolling off the production lines for them to be made available to various support functions. In July 1942 at Camp Young, Indio, California, a jeep is used as transportation for Red Cross representatives.

The jeep became so popular with general officers that early in 1942 the army set up a two-week school at Fort Holabird, Maryland, to teach them the vehicle's handling and maintenance features. Among the first general officers through the course were (*left to right*) Brig. Gens. Vernon E. Prichard of the 4th Armored Division at Pine Camp, New York, T. E. Marchant of the 30th Infantry Division at Fort Jackson, South Carolina, and Joseph C. Hutchinson of the 21st Infantry Division at Fort Blanding, Florida.

An annotated photograph of the inside front of the jeep that appeared in *Life* magazine early in the war.

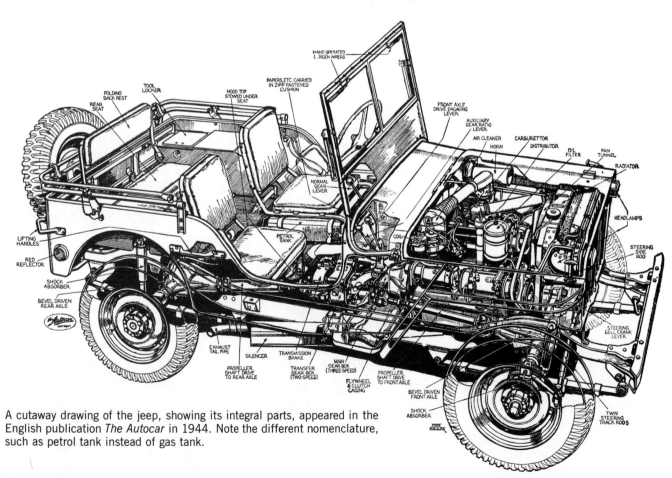

A cutaway drawing of the jeep, showing its integral parts, appeared in the English publication *The Autocar* in 1944. Note the different nomenclature, such as petrol tank instead of gas tank.

The first use of a jeep in an amphibious landing took place at a 1st Division landing operation in North Carolina.

When rivers were too deep and there was no time to build temporary bridges, other means were devised to move the jeeps across.

Above: Jeeps in New Caledonia in the South Pacific in July 1942 going through combat-readiness maneuvers.

In a publicity picture, three Civil War veterans attending a 1942 reunion at Fort Oglethorpe, Georgia, try out the new jeep (*Life* magazine).

2

THE JEEP IN WORLD WAR II —EUROPE

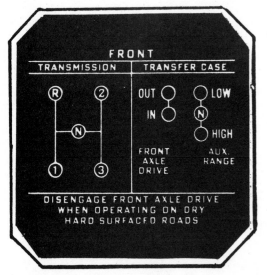

Each jeep contained an instruction plate that explained the proper operation of the 3-speed transmission gears and the 4-wheel drive. These plates were also printed in three other languages—Russian, Chinese, and Spanish.

The first primary use of the jeep in wartime was in its deployment to Europe, starting in the British Isles and then in North Africa.

How was the jeep to be employed in the army as a tactical vehicle? Long before the jeep went into mass production by Willys and Ford, the army had set up many of its tactical needs in the military specifications expressed for it. For example, the low silhouette, the 4-wheel drive, and the drop frame for the chassis were experimented with, proved practical, and developed into working models long before being incorporated into the vehicle itself.

For the army, the jeep replaced the cavalry horse, just as the motor vehicle replaced the horse and buggy. The birth of the automobile at the turn of the century and its finite engineering development in the 1920s outmoded the cavalry horse in the 1930s. Starting in 1922, the army began to minimize its cavalry and was desperately in search of a vehicle that would better than approximate the cross-country ability of the horse. The cavalry search was for a vehicle that could perform reconnaissance off roads, carry more than one man as well as weapons and ammunition, be used for communications, have a relatively low profile, and be quiet. Horses could jump ditches while motor vehicles known at that time could not. And the army seekers knew that all the way back to the Civil War for Americans—and further back for other nations—battles had been lost because reconnaissance soldiers on horseback had had their mounts shot out from under them and were not able to return to their own lines. What was

Many wartime notables were photographed in the jeep. The president of the United States, Franklin D. Roosevelt, reviews the troops at Casablanca in North Africa. The driver is Sgt. Oran Lass and at the far left is Lt. Gen. (later Gen.) Mark Clark.

British Prime Minister Winston Churchill lights a cigar while in a jeep, observing the Normandy landing operations. With him is Gen. (later Field Marshal) Bernard Montgomery.

A front view of the 1942 Ford version of the jeep. During World War II, Willys-Overland built 359,849 jeeps and Ford built 227,314, under a Willys license.

His Britannic Majesty King George VI (left) inspecting one of the lend-lease jeeps while on an inspection trip in England.

needed was a reconnaissance vehicle that could be counted on to return.

At that time the infantry also became interested in finding a similar vehicle. Both the infantry and the cavalry tried using the motorcycle, but even with a sidecar, it did not meet all, or enough, of the requirements. Both branches also experimented (unsuccessfully) with various kinds of tractors. In 1932, the search was accelerated after the army, using horses, had trouble putting down a march of unemployed veterans on Washington, D.C. By 1937, the army's top strategists and tacticians were concluding that what they needed was a "1/4-ton, 4-wheel-drive, low-profile, powerful vehicle."

Both infantry and cavalry officers wanted a mechanized vehicle, rather than a horse, for the periods when they were out in front, leading their troops. General Douglas MacArthur had stated, during the 1932 veterans' march, that the horse should be replaced by a motor vehicle for the commanding officer in such situations. "A cavalry mount of this sort [the horse] will never work in modern wartime," he said. "The value of the cavalry ended with the Spanish American War."

Jeeps are leading a caravan of camels past the Sphinx and Pyramids near Cairo, Egypt, during a special recreational activity for airmen on leave in North Africa in December 1942.

At Camp Huckstep near Cairo, Egypt, in 1942 an ingenious GI uses water from a jeep's radiator to whip up hot lather for a shave.

A jeep brings back three GIs who were trapped by German gunfire for three days at Kasserine Pass in North Africa in February 1943.

The army visionaries had their dreams fulfilled in 1941 with the advent of the jeep. The first combat tests it was put to—in North Africa and Europe—proved that it met the specifications the infantry and cavalry commanders had set for it.

The jeeps were employed first of all to support the infantrymen's advance. Once the infantrymen and/or tanks gained the military objective, the jeeps could effect immediate forward displacement of automatic weapons, infantry mortars, antitank guns, ammunition, and communications, in order to consolidate the position and quickly set up for the next advance.

Both the American GIs and their officers had a romance with the jeep in World War II. Fortunately the new vehicles were in sufficient supply to be everywhere, and it seemed as though every U.S. soldier had one. Two stories that were told about this love match are worth repeating.

The first is set in North Africa. One night in a combat zone, a Free French soldier on sentry duty at point A challenged three soldiers in American uniforms coming through a checkpoint. One of the three said they were Americans walking to point A from point B, five miles distant. The French sentry cocked his rifle and told them to put up their hands. They started to flee, and the sentry shot them dead. After the excitement died down and the

18

Movie stars (*left to right*) Carol Landis, Kay Francis, and Martha Raye on a United Services Organization (USO) tour in North Africa ask for directions while traveling from one point to another to entertain the troops. This photograph received so much publicity in the United States that in 1944 a motion picture was produced about the USO tours, entitled *Four Jills in a Jeep.* The fourth "Jill" was Mitzi Mayfair.

A German "jeep" is brought back in 1943 to the Aberdeen Proving Ground in Maryland for comparison tests with its American counterpart. The German Volkswagen, captured in the North African desert, came in a poor second.

"Americans" were identified as German infiltrators, the Frenchman was asked how he knew they weren't Americans. He replied, "One, they weren't riding in a jeep—all American GIs ride in jeeps—and two, he said they walked five miles. The American doesn't walk even one avenue, he rides."

The second story took place during the Battle of the Bulge. A Belgian sentry at a checkpoint stopped a jeep bearing three soldiers in American uniforms and immediately ordered them in German to surrender. Later, when asked how he knew they were Germans, the sentry said, "One, the colonel was riding in back and the aide was driving. The real American colonel drives and the aide rides next to him. Besides, the American colonel never rides in back because it gives them what you call 'it'—the piles."

As the jeep became more plentiful in the European Theater of Operations, it was used for many other missions and roles in addition to its tactical employment.

A great number of jeeps were used by the U.S. Army Air Force in England in conjunction with air operations and as ground support. A military police jeep and its occupants are on their way into London in 1943 in an early morning patrol to find stragglers returning to the air bases for the next day's missions.

In Italy, in 1944, the air force used jeeps for rapid turnaround in air combat missions. Pilots of Lockheed P-38 "Lightning" fighter planes speed back to their 94th Fighter Squadron operations room for debriefing.

A jeep with a portable radio set being loaded aboard a C-47 in England for transport to France shortly after D-Day, June 1944.

S. Sgt. Stanley Brown of Richmond, Virginia (*at wheel*), developed this version of the jeep while with the 15th Air Force in Italy. Brown was an ordnance worker with a Consolidated B-24 "Liberator" group in 1944.

Backing a jeep into a glider can be a tight fit. Many jeeps were flown from England to France this way.

The soldier at the wheel ready to drive off on landing.

"Somewhere in France," a jeep is unloaded from a Douglas C-47 Skytrain. The Skytrains, which hauled the gliders, also carried a cargo of jeeps.

At an ordnance depot in southern England, armor plate was welded onto the front of this jeep so it could be used to push stalled vehicles.

In a scene typical of an English air base early in 1944, a radio-equipped jeep serves as a mobile "control tower" at the ends of a runway to facilitate the operation of a combat mission.

Another example of American ingenuity: When wet weather threatened to slow down the jeeps in Luxembourg late in 1944, Capt. L. S. Rainhart of the 981st Engineer Maintenance Company designed a "mud shoe" which allowed the vehicles to slide and float through the sludge.

A communications jeep passes an abandoned German wagon and dead horse in the Remoncourt area of France in December 1944. By this time the Germans were using many horses to pull their supply wagons.

21

In a rare photograph, Russian officials come out in lend-lease jeeps to greet one of the first Consolidated B-24 Liberators to land at Poltava, Soviet Union, in 1944.

A Catholic chaplain in France uses the hood of a jeep as an altar to say Mass for men of the 90th Division in late 1944.

Capt. D. A. Thomas, with the U.S. Army Air Forces who had just arrived at Poltava in 1944, discusses the merits of the jeep with a Russian driver. The Russians tended to use jeeps as personnel carriers rather than for other uses in combat areas.

Eupen, Belgium, January 1945: A member of the 127th Ordnance Maintenance Batallion of the 5th U.S. Armored Division converted this jeep, 2 feet 6 inches longer than the standard models, into an eight-man personnel carrier.

Members of the 39th Signal Construction Battalion of the 9th U.S. Army Division used parts from wrecked jeeps, a French automobile, and a German airplane to construct this multipurpose jeep somewhere in France in December 1944. The rubber tires were interchangeable with a special rim which made it possible to run the vehicle on a standard-gauge railway.

T/5 Peter Pupporo of Oswego, New York, driver for a station hospital in Florence, Italy, winterized his jeep for the ambulatory patients in the winter of 1944. Many a GI during the war saw the jeep in his charge as his own private vehicle.

Another jeep that was altered to ride on both land roads and railroads. Note the four tires stored on the side. More than 100 jeeps were altered in this way in 1944 and 1945, since U.S. airpower had destroyed nearly every European railroad engine on the drive to Germany.

Two soldiers of the 3rd Armored Division hurrying in a jeep toward the front lines in Worms, Germany, in March 1945 pass a burning German truck, one of many along the road that were destroyed by the 3rd Army's armored field artillery.

At Bastogne, Belgium, in January 1945, a jeep is pressed into service as a snowplow with the addition of a sheet of curved steel. Jeeps were called on to perform many tasks beyond their design mission due to the exigencies of war.

The 13th Infantry Regiment of the 8th Infantry Division had to use jeeps as ammunition haulers when bigger trucks were not available in January 1945. A jeep pulls an ammunition sled in the snow near Hurtgen, Germany.

Lt. Gen. Omar N. Bradley, Commanding General, 12th Army Group, pauses in his jeep tour of the First Army's divisions to sign autographs for the GIs, February 19, 1945. To his right is Maj. Gen. J. Lawton Collins, Commanding General, 3rd Armored Division.

Maj. Gen. Maxwell D. Taylor, commanding general of the 101st Airborne Division, uses the hood of his jeep as a podium to welcome reinforcements at Neuss, Germany, early in 1945.

President Franklin D. Roosevelt, arriving at Saki Airport, Crimea, Russia, in February 1945, engages in conversation with England's prime minister, Winston Churchill, on their way to the Yalta Conference.

The jeep assigned to Gen. George S. Patton in the closing days of World War II. The story that Patton was killed in a jeep accident is untrue. He died December 9, 1945, in an automobile accident while riding as a passenger in his staff car, a Cadillac limousine.

3

THE JEEP IN *YANK* MAGAZINE, WORLD WAR II

Yank, the prestigious, official army weekly of World War II, was written solely by enlisted men exclusively for the enlisted man—the GI. (The Department of Defense still publishes one issue each year to keep the trademark in the government domain.) Probably the best way to explain the difference in audiences between enlisted men and the officers is to use as an example the book *See Here, Private Hargrove*, a novel about the army that was written to depict the class differences between the GIs and the officers. Hargrove, a sergeant on the staff of *Yank*, had written the book earlier. While with *Yank*, however, he did not write "a word that was for any other group than the GI." Also, the famous novelist Irwin Shaw, when joining *Yank* as a private, said that it was like "starting [writing] all over again."

This unique journalistic approach worked well, probably because enlisted men knew best the sort of writing the GIs needed for their enjoyment and to keep up their morale. The enlisted writers not only knew the GI language, they were aware that the GIs hated KP, K-rations, "second looies," the army's table of organization that lim-

ited promotions, good conduct ribbons, the rotation plan for return to the States, "USO (United Services Organizations) commandos" who hung out at the service clubs, and, most of all, the "off limits" places that the officers staked out for themselves.

Except for the jeep, for which both groups shared an enthusiasm, there was a definite difference in outlook between the enlisted men and the officers. On the other hand, the GI writers on *Yank* knew that the enlisted man yearned most of all to return to the basics of life at home: the family, good food, the girl friend, peace and quiet, and that singular American passion, his own personal automobile. The jeep served to satisfy the latter desire. The enlisted men felt that the 4-wheel-drive vehicle was a GIs' car. More enlisted men lost a stripe for "borrowing" a jeep in the combat zone than for any other offense.

Therefore it was no accident that the *Yank* writers placed considerable emphasis on putting the jeep into the copy of the magazine. This special effort, in turn, doubtless played a major role in the returning GIs being prominent among the purchasers of the peacetime jeep.

"The Sad Sack" by Sgt. George Baker, *Yank* magazine

YANK *The Army Newspaper* • SEPTEMBER 30

"The Message."

YANK *The Army Weekly* • OCTOBER 19, 1945

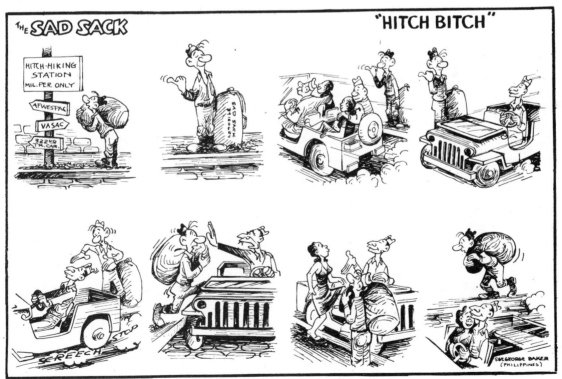

"Hitch Bitch."

"Lush Living."

"Rank Injustice."

Yank was published every week between the summer of 1942 and August 1945, when the war ended. All the issues were prepared by enlisted men, without a single contribution from a noncommissioned officer, a warrant officer, or a commissioned officer. Enlisted men who became officers usually moved over to the daily *Stars & Stripes*, which to the staff of *Yank* was "just like any other daily newspaper."

The jeep salutes *Yank* magazine!

German jeep inferior.

Jeeps on the mail run.

Rescued after three weeks afloat on a raft in the Pacific, Capt. Eddie Rickenbacker was still able to show a grin as he sat in a jeep. Six other members of plane crew were also saved.

Capt. Eddie Rickenbacker rescued.

YANK The Army Weekly • MARCH 19

"Road to Kokumbona"

The Last Days at Guadalcanal

The "Road to Kokumbona"—the last days at Guadalcanal.

30

YANK
THE ARMY WEEKLY

5¢

SEPT. 21, 1945
VOL. 4, NO. 14

By and for men in the service

CIVILIAN JEEP

German SS Women Let Down Hair In PW Camp

PAGES 10 & 11

The civilian jeep.

CIVILIAN JEEP

THE MODEL THEY HAVE DREAMED UP FOR THE POSTWAR TRADE IS FANCIER — BUT IT STILL LOOKS LIKE A JEEP

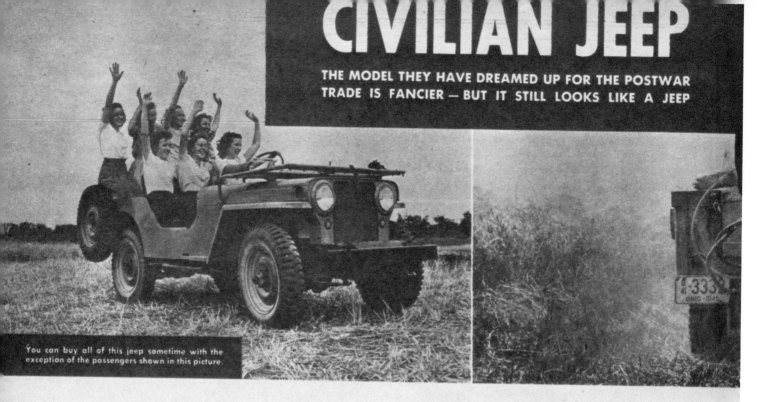

You can buy all of this jeep sometime with the exception of the passengers shown in this picture.

By Sgt. JAMES P. O'NEILL
YANK Staff Writer

TOLEDO, OHIO—On a farm in Hudson County, Mich., the little blitz buggy of World War II, the jeep, donned civilian clothes and, just like most GIs, looked a helluva lot better out of ODs.

Willys-Overland, which is taking a keen, commercial interest in helping the jeep to make the switch-over from Army to civilian life, put 30 of the new models through their paces. Before a large crowd of farmers, soldiers and newspapermen the new jeep positively failed to whistle "Lili Marlene" in C sharp minor.

But judging by what went on out here in Michigan, the jeep may become as familiar around the farm as that Castoria ad on the barn roof. The jeep has seen Paree, and some other places, but according to its sponsors, the farm is the place where it is chiefly going to keep itself down on in this postwar era.

Government surveys have unearthed the fact that three-fourths of the nation's farms lack mechanical equipment. The jeep, its manufacturers say, combines the basic functions of a tractor, a light truck, a mobile power unit and a utility car. They reason, accordingly, that it will be the answer to the farmer's prayer. At the demonstration there was at least one farmer who agreed with them. "I wanted to buy one just outta curiosity," he said, "but after what I've seen today I ain't curious. That little car's goin' to be a lifesaver."

The most significant change in the civilian jeep is the new power take-off attachment. This gadget, geared to the jeep's transmission, will drive any type of farming equipment. With the take-off attached, here are some of the things a jeep can do: It can shred corn, fill a silo, operate a winch, dig post holes, drill water wells, bale hay and operate a saw mill—with, of course, the aid of human hands. On all of these operations it can deliver up to 30 hp.

The new jeep has the same engine as its brother in ODs, but the gear ratios in the transmission and axles have been changed. With the new gear ratio the jeep can reputedly adapt itself to any type of farming terrain and to any speed that the job may require. The jeep can slow down to a farm pace of 7.5 miles an hour or go spinning down the highway at 60. It positively cannot outdistance the P-80 Shooting Star, however.

Optimists estimate that the jeep can perform more than 45 different operations on the farm. They say they can prove their case on the basis of the records the civilian jeep has hung up in tests at experimental farm stations in the U.S. and Canada.

In Texas the jeep rode the range and checked stock—or rather the man in it checked stock, the jeep being unable to count as yet—in half an hour; ordinarily, the chore required half a day. In a rice field in Arkansas, where the combination of dykes and levees and gumbo-like

The power take-off attachment, geared to the jeep's transmission, will operate a buzz saw.

Here, with jeep's tail board down, is the power attachment, to make milk-shakes or cut trees.

A very effective sprayer can be attached to the rear of the car for the benefit of your fruit trees.

Another asset of the new jeep is its pulling power. This one pulls a disc harrow behind it.

soil makes plowing extremely tough, the jeep negotiated the narrow rows with no trouble.

In contour plowing in upstate New York the jeep maintained its equilibrium; thanks to the four-wheel drive it never jammed the earth. In a western state the U. S. Forestry Service is using two jeeps as a team to fight fires. One jeep carries a crew of four men and the other jeep hauls the water tank, power pump and hand tools.

The uses of the postwar jeep, its sponsors claim, won't be limited to farming and fire-fighting. With its handy power take-off and other attachments the jeep can be employed to operate small electric plants, move railroad yard freight and plow snow. And it may possibly invade the trucking business—a jeep will pull a trailer load of 5,500 pounds over the highway with adequate reserve for steep grades.

Without a doubt, the jeep, in off-hours, will be one of the biggest boons of all to the postwar cupid industry. With a jeep, lovers can be assured of privacy. As one wise guy, apparently a friend of a farmer's daughter, said at the demonstration: "The jeep can take me and my girl so far out of this world that we will have to get back by compass."

Willys-Overland, however, does not intend to use this particular plug in its postwar advertising.

Most of the innovations in the civilian jeep are aimed at achieving all-around usefulness. A new combustion chamber has been designed to give increased power, and there is a new radiator shroud that will provide better cooling for long-stretch low-speed driving on farms. The clutch is larger and has been reinforced and the gear shift now sits on the steering wheel, making the front seats much roomier. With linkage changes, the jeep handles much more easily and takes a much sharper turn than the GI version.

Despite all the changes, the jeep looks much the same and you won't be mistaking it for a Mack truck. There is one change you will like simply for its labor-saving value. When you want to fill up with gas you don't have to get out of the car and lift up the driver's seat to get at the gas cap. On the civilian jeep the gas cap is on the outside, just behind the driver's seat. The jeep now has standard 7-inch headlights, an automatic windshield wiper, a tail gate.

Willys-Overland officials have got round to giving some thought to the posteriors of jeep drivers. They've finally taken cognizance of the terrific wallop a jeep bounce can pack and have installed better shock absorbers and springs. The seats on the civilian jeep are padded with nice, fat cushions.

At the demonstration here a GI who had driven a jeep over Italy's rugged mountains for 18 months kept patting the cushions as if they were precious antiques. "From here on in," the GI said, "I can look at a jeep without getting a pain in the backside, like I used to get in Italy."

Two companies—Willys-Overland and Ford—were responsible for the 500,000 Army jeeps that traveled over 10 billion miles during the war. Ford stopped military production in July and has no intention of making jeeps for civilian use. But civilian jeeps have been trickling off the Willys-Overland production line in Toledo at the rate of eight a day. Until the war in the Pacific was over, the company's main job was to furnish jeeps to the forces out there. Before VJ-Day the company got War Production Board permission to make 20,000 civilian jeeps this year, 70,000 next year. With the war over, civilian production should rise.

The price of the civilian jeep will surprise a lot of people who thought this midget would be an inexpensive postwar item. A jeep without accessories will cost $1,050, f. o. b. Toledo. The best things in life continue to require an awful lot of folding money.

The jeep, though, will save money on gasoline.

On the road, its sponsors say, it will get a minimum of 20 miles to a gallon of gas, and in a farm test the jeep plowed 400 acres at an hourly rate of 1¼ acres, consuming only two gallons of gas each hour.

Officials asked the GIs present at the Hudson County demonstration to squawk if they didn't like anything about the new jeep. One GI came through with a very constructive criticism. "You don't have 'em painted in enough colors," he complained.

"We have them in gray, tan, blue and brown," a hurt company man pointed out. "Don't these colors give enough variety?"

"They do not," said the doughfoot. "Paint 'em pink, purple and orange. Paint 'em any color you like but get as far away from that lousy OD shade as possible. Personally, I want a pink one."

The manufacturers think the dough may have something there. How do you want your jeep—in cerise or violet?

DO YOU WANT TO OWN ONE?

Before the Jap surrender a YANK *man asked that question of a number of jeep drivers in motor pools around Manila. The answers printed here represent a cross section of how the GIs felt. Most of them thought a postwar jeep would come in very handy. A few wouldn't be seen dead in one, but perhaps a dressed-up civilian jeep will change their minds.*

Pvt. Bill Kramer of Grand Rapids, Mich., used to be an Infantryman in the 32d Division. After the battle of Buna, he was transferred from the Infantry and put in a base-section motor pool. Kramer has been a driver and a dispatcher ever since. He answers the question this way: "Not interested! Why? Well, guess I've ridden in 'em over too many of those rough New Guinea roads."

Pfc. Edward Kaminiski of Jersey City, N. J., is in an Antitank company of the 37th Division. His outfit helped take Manila. Ed was driving a radio traffic control jeep in the Manila area while his outfit was on MP duty resting up between operations. Kaminiski used to be a truck driver before he joined the Infantry and says: "Sure I want one. Will be a lot more fun driving the wife and kid around on Sundays in a jeep than in an ordinary car. The parking problem in Jersey and New York is no picnic; the jeep will be a cinch to sneak into a small space. The back seat is a hell of a fine Mother-in-Law seat too."

Pfc. Eugene George comes from Du Quoin, Ill., and has seen all he wants to see of New Guinea, Leyte and Luzon. When he gets back home, he says, a jeep will be just the thing for him. "I live in the country where the roads are really rough. A jeep will be a life saver for driving to and from my work in the city."

Pfc. Edward Turnbull hails from Tucson, Ariz., and is a veteran of the Buna fighting with the 32d Division. Ed, an experienced jeep driver, says: "Yes, I can think of a thousand uses for one, but most important out of the thousand is the help they'll be on the range. Why, one jeep will be able to replace several horses in the tough job of repairing breaks in the fences on the range and they'll make getting around the desert a hell of a lot easier too."

Wac Pfc. Margie Michael of Akron, Ohio, is doing a lot of driving for the WAC around Manila these days. Margie was in war work before joining the WAC and has driven overseas on Leyte and Luzon. She says: "A jeep fits me. I learned to drive on a jeep, and I'd like to have one after the war because they are easy to drive and park. Some people complain about the seats, but I like them just the way they are."

YANK THE ARMY WEEKLY

CARTOONS

The original of the famous Bill Mauldin cartoon of the old cavalry sergeant shooting his mortally wounded horse.

"LOOK, YOU GUYS—A PONTIAC!"

—Cpl. Frank R. Robinson

CPL. PETE & HIS JEEP—

"Oh, fudge."
—Sgt. Douglas Borgstedt

—Sgt. Bob Bowie, Bolling Field, D. C.

4

THE JEEP IN WORLD WAR II —THE PACIFIC

Although jeeps were introduced at the U.S. military installations in the Pacific long before the attack at Pearl Harbor on December 7, 1941, it was not until 1943 that they appeared in great numbers in the Pacific islands and Asia. Early in 1943 the drive began to regain the territories lost to the Japanese after Pearl Harbor. The first military pushes into Burma and throughout the islands in the Pacific required that the jeep be employed in many different roles.

The mission of the jeep in the Pacific was different from the tactical role it played in the European theater. In the Pacific the jeep was mainly the tool of support operations in combat and support services behind the lines. The Army Corps of Engineers used it extensively for advance transportation for its engineers in bridge and road building.

The jeep also served in many other miscellaneous roles. Not unlike its use in Europe, it became the personal staff car of commanding officers and the main mode of transportation of the GIs—when they could get their hands on one. It became the standard form of reliable transportation throughout the Pacific and the China Burma India Theater, where it served well despite the constant storms and rain that made the dirt roads almost impassable.

Originally designed as a reconnaissance vehicle, the jeep with its six speeds forward and two in reverse became a jack-of-all-trades. Mounted with a .50-caliber machine gun, the highly versatile 4-wheel-drive vehicle raised havoc with snipers and enemy in general who were constantly harassing Allied soldiers and strafing the airdromes. Jeeps were used to haul

Above left: Gen. Douglas MacArthur in the front seat of a jeep on his way to review the combat operations in New Guinea (1944). The driver is Lt. Gen. Robert L. Eichelberger.

Left: The U.S. Army's chief of staff, Gen. George C. Marshall, seated in the front of a jeep while observing jungle warfare training in the Hawaiian Islands (1944). The driver is Lt. Col. W. C. Saffarrans and the officer in the rear seat is Lt. Gen. Robert C. Richardson.

Gen. Joseph W. Stilwell uses a jeep train while touring the Myitkyina battle area in Burma on July 18, 1944.

Below: The Supreme Allied Commander in Asia, Lord Louis Mountbatten, regularly rode the jeep railroad between Mogaung and Sahmaw in Burma (1944).

Lord Louis Mountbatten on an inspection in Burma in December 1944. The driver of the jeep is Maj. Gen. C. N. Wood, the commanding general of the Indian 25th Division.

and tow heavy equipment, and as field ambulances and stretcher bearers. Among their countless official tasks were some extracurricular ones, the flat hood being used by GIs as a dining table or by chaplains as altars.

The officers and GIs in the Pacific were just as innovative as their counterparts in Europe in converting and adapting the jeep to countless other roles, such as employing it as transportation on the railroads.

Although all of the top commanders lauded the jeep's versatility, it was Maj. Gen. Eugene Reybold, the World War II U.S. Army chief of engineers, who wrapped it all up by saying, ''I have seen the jeep everywhere, and though it is doubtless mere coincidence, for there must be many disabled or wrecked jeeps, I myself in all my travels have never seen a jeep that would not run when it was needed.''

Toward the end of the war in both the European and Asian theaters, the jeep, having served its combat role, was converted to a support vehicle in countless service roles. In the final days, as the war wound down, the jeep was being converted into civilian roles on the farms, in transportation, in fire-control services, and commercially as a passenger car or a truck.

In the space of one war—one big war—the jeep had managed to replace the horse and the tractor and become a passenger car as well.

Gen. Joseph W. Stilwell fording a river with his jeep on his way to the front in northern Burma, Easter Sunday, 1944. Note the general's trademark campaign hat up front in the lead jeep. The jeeps are using chains on all four tires for the 4-wheel drive across the river.

38

In Burma in 1944, the GIs went their European brothers in arms one better and built their own railroad operated by jeeps supplying the locomotion. A jeep is being slid off a siding to be put on the main track.

A jeep locomotive pulling a flatcar in Burma in 1944.

Brig. Gen. C. W. Connell, Commanding General, Air Services Command, Brisbane, Australia, drives a jeep fitted with rail wheels to pull a flatcar weighing 20,000 pounds. The jeep was converted for duty in New Guinea.

Philippines, early Spring 1945: An engineer officer stations his jeep at the front of the construction battalion where he can best supervise the road building. The Engineer battalions used the jeeps more than any other group of soldiers.

A convoy of jeep ambulances evacuates the wounded from the beaches of Iwo Jima while the fighting is still going on in March 1945.

The mud on New Britain island in the South Pacific could only be conquered by the jeep (1945).

A jeep being unloaded from a C-47 Skytrain at a base in Burma, in early 1945. In Asia, jeeps had to be flown by airplane and glider since the distance from rear-echelon depots in India to forward bases was too great to drive them and the engineers had not yet completed the roads.

An engineering officer supervises a construction crew putting a pass through a mountain range in Tibet in June 1945.

Members of the Mexican Expeditionary Air Force in the Philippines during World War II crowd into a jeep after their first combat mission with the 5th Air Force's 58th Fighter Group (1945). Several of them voiced the opinion that the vehicle would be very popular in Mexico after the war.

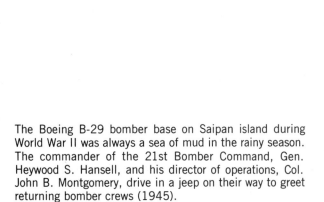

In front of the nose of their Consolidated B-24 Liberator bomber, the "Lil Audrey," the pilot, 1st Lt. Francis Rouls of Pasadena, California, stands on the hood of a jeep to brief the crew on their 100th and last mission for the 7th Air Force in the Pacific in 1945. The crews had jeeps assigned to them for quicker transportation in mission support.

The Boeing B-29 bomber base on Saipan island during World War II was always a sea of mud in the rainy season. The commander of the 21st Bomber Command, Gen. Heywood S. Hansell, and his director of operations, Col. John B. Montgomery, drive in a jeep on their way to greet returning bomber crews (1945).

A jeep used for "follow-me" duty leads a landed Boeing B-29 bomber to its hardstand (parking place) (1945).

By the war's end the Willys-Overland production line in Toledo, Ohio, was turning out jeeps at the rate of three every four minutes, twenty-four hours a day, seven days a week. The last wartime jeep was built in Toledo on August 20, 1945.

Riding in a jeep after their arrival at Luzon, Philippines, Japanese general Tomoyuki Yamashita and two members of his staff are on their way to Baguio to sign the official surrender papers marking the end of the war, September 2, 1945.

5

POST-WORLD WAR II JEEPS

Jeep CJ-2A (1946). Production of a peacetime "Universal" jeep began as soon as war ended, and thousands were sold to farmers for use as tractors and trucks. Serial numbers for the 1,824 CJ-2As built in 1945 were 10,001–11,824; those for the 71,554 models turned out in 1946, 11,825–83,379.

The Willys-Overland Corporation started a civilian vehicle production line rolling before the war officially ended. Nearly 2,000 CJ-2A models were built in 1945. GIs from all services had expressed a strong desire to have their own jeep when they got out of uniform. Once the soldiers, sailors, and airmen returned home and to their jobs, Willys couldn't build the vehicle fast enough to meet the demand for them. Jeeps were also needed for farms, in businesses, and in all sorts of commercial operations. As a result, the jeep became a station wagon, a tractor, and a truck.

By mid-1946, sales were going so well for the CJ model that by the end of the year Willys had produced 71,000 of them. So great was the clamor from the public for a civilian version of the wartime jeep that Willys set up a production line for a jeep station wagon. Sales were brisk, and the company reopened its wartime West Coast plant. By the end of 1947, they had produced more than 60,000 of the station wagons.

Willys then added 2- and 4-wheel-drive pickup and panel trucks to their lines. With all going well, the decision was made to enter the more popular markets with a convertible "Jeepster" sports phaeton in 1949. Although the phaeton was very popular in 1949 and 1950, it did not reach a high enough sales level to become a staple vehicle in the marketplace.

The jeep station wagon continued to sell well. In the end, however, the old military jeep design came back to rescue the company when overall sales dropped. The armed forces continued to buy jeeps as replacements for the pre-war and early World War II jeeps that were finally getting too old for military use.

Then, in the 1950–1952 period, the U.S. Army ordered 60,000 of the new Willys design for the jeep—the M-38. Again the army had foresight that paid off. The new vehicles came off the production lines just in time to see combat duty in the Korean Conflict.

By the end of November 1945, the Steyr plant in Vienna, Austria, was turning out twenty-five winterized jeeps each day in what was probably the most efficient military effort worldwide to weatherproof the jeeps. A winterized jeep coming off the assembly line contrasts vividly with an open one about to enter the Steyr plant.

When U.S. forces occupied Japan after the war, the jeep became a common sight in Japanese cities, offering a sharp contrast to the pedal-driven rickshaw.

A rodeo put on by the military command in Tokyo in November 1945 would not have been complete without a demonstration of jeep-jumping.

Jeep model 463 (1946). On July 11, 1946, Willys began producing an all-steel jeep seven-passenger station wagon, an industry first. A total of 6,534 were built in the first year.

Army Chief of Staff Gen. Dwight D. Eisenhower in the back seat of a jeep on a tour of Kyoto during an inspection trip to Japan in 1946. In the front are Lt. Gen. Robert Eichelberger (*left*) and Maj. Gen. Roscoe B. Woodruff (*driving*).

At its air bases in the Southwest, the U.S. Air Force developed a jeep equipped with radio, fire-fighting equipment, and a fence-cutting apparatus for response to off-base fires (1946).

Willys-Overland had a banner year in 1947, with sales topping every year since 1928. Champagne flowed as the company reopened its West Coast plant at Los Angeles. CJ-2A models accounted for 65,078 of the total of 119,477 jeep vehicles built (serial numbers 83,380–148,458).

Jeep truck (1947). Production began in the spring of 1947 on all-new jeep pickup and panel delivery trucks. Included were a 2-wheel-drive general-purpose model on a 118-inch wheelbase (2,642 units produced) and a 104-inch-wheelbase panel delivery (2,346 units).

Jeepster model VJ-2 (1949). In May 1948, Willys-Overland began producing the Jeepster sports phaeton, now widely recognized as a collectible, special-interest vehicle. A total of 12,633 of the 1949 models with a vertical grille were built. Despite record production of 136,648 vehicles in 1948, there was a sharp drop in total 1949 production, to 83,250 units. The CJ-3A replaced the CJ-2A after 1949.

Jeepster model VJ-3 (1950). A new horizontal grille and other refinements distinguished the 1950 Jeepster, which by that year was available with both 4- and 6-cylinder engines. Vehicles for the calendar year totaled 86,716, up slightly from 1949. Jeep CJ-3A models accounted for 26,035 of the total.

The air force in 1950 found the jeep the best form of transportation for its remote radar stations in the far north and Alaska. Able to climb hills and mountains to the sites in all kinds of weather, radar-site jeeps often acquired a winter coating.

Jeep station wagon (1950). On March 3, 1950, Willys-Overland staged a big dealer meeting in Toledo to announce new models featuring new front-end styling and two new engines, the Hurricane F-head 4 and the Lightning L-head 6. A new 1/2-ton 2-wheel-drive truck was also introduced.

In 1950 the army announced that it was developing a new, more powerful, improved model of the jeep, the M-38. Five inches longer and two inches wider than the existing models, it was powered with a 72-hp F-head engine in place of the standard 60-hp L-head. With improved fuel economy and larger gasoline tanks, the new model had a range of 300 miles without refueling as compared to the old range of 180 miles. A snorkel device that comes in a kit could be attached in 15 minutes.

In 1950–1952, Willys-Overland built 60,345 M-38 4-wheel-drive military vehicles for the U.S. Army. An improved version of the wartime MB, they featured higher ground clearance, maximum gradability of 65 percent, a 24-volt electrical system, and deep fording capability. The new jeep cost less, rode better, and had more power and a greater cruising range. The hood was raised to accommodate the new engine.

49

Exercise Long Horn, Fort Hood, Texas, 1952. The regimental commander pointing to the seven-foot-long horns for which the exercise is named is Col. Robert P. Miller, 136th Infantry ("Bearcat") Regiment.

Soldiers of the 82nd Airborne Division untie a jeep that has just landed by parachute during Exercise Long Horn. Landing of jeeps by parachute for the 82nd Airborne had become a routine operation.

During this period the U.S. Air Force continued to use its old communications jeep with the air force aerial demonstration team, the Thunderbirds.

In 1952 the air force developed a portable lubrication and maintenance assembly to suspend jeeps for servicing.

Military jeeps get a workout all over the world almost daily, in different employments. In Germany in 1953, two soldiers operate M-38 jeeps that have been equipped with bulldozer blades for filling ditches.

Everywhere during the Korean Conflict, jeeps were being reconditioned for possible use in combat. At the Germersheim Ordnance Vehicle Park in Germany, over a thousand jeeps were reconditioned.

A demonstration of the snorkel on an M-38 jeep at Fort Sill, Oklahoma, in 1959.

THE JEEP IN THE KOREAN CONFLICT

The updated M-38 model of the jeep developed by Willys and the U.S. Army Ordnance Corps surfaced just in time and was procured in sufficient numbers to be of great use to the military in the Korean Conflict.

The Korean Conflict began on June 25, 1950, when South Korea was invaded by North Korean Communist forces. Many nations of the free world joined forces with South Korea and the United States and, as the United Nations Command, fought the Communist North Korean and Chinese forces until an armistice was signed on July 27, 1953.

The tactical use of the jeep in Korea differed from its employment in World War II. Even though the nearly totally mountainous terrain of North Korea might have logically influenced the army to minimize

In 1947 the 6th Reconnaissance Unit, stationed in Korea, was ready to move out on patrol with its jeeps and armored scout cars.

Gen. of the Army Douglas MacArthur, Commander-in-Chief, UN Forces in Korea, and Maj. Gen. Oliver P. Smith, Commanding General, 1st Marine Division, depart on a tour of the Yellow Beach area at Inchon, Korea, September 17, 1950.

The 7th Cavalry Regiment of the 1st Cavalry Division are given an orientation lecture by their commanding officer, Col. Cecil Nist, before being sent to the front lines. Loudspeakers and amplifiers were frequently hooked up to a jeep's power source to be used in field operations.

Maj. Edward M. Almond, Commanding General, X Corps, drives his jeep down to the harbor at Hungnam on Christmas Eve, 1950, to confer with Maj. Robert H. Soule, commanding general of the 3rd Infantry Division, during the late hours of the evacuation of United Nations troops from the Hungnam area.

Lt. Gen. Matthew B. Ridgway (*front seat*), newly appointed commanding general of the 8th U.S. Army, and Maj. Gen. Frank W. Milburn (*back seat*), Commanding General, I Corps, leave in a jeep for an inspection of the front lines, December 27, 1950.

Periodic maintenance of jeep engines was important in combat because of the rough terrain in Korea and the extensive use of the 4-wheel-drive vehicle.

the use of the jeep, this did not turn out to be the case. Many new support roles directly related to combat became standard requirements for the reliable 4-wheel-drive vehicle. The jeep spearheaded the strategic withdrawal from the north when, in October 1950, the Chinese entered the war. And once the fighting began along a static 140-mile line at the 38th parallel, the jeep started to play all kinds of new combat and support roles in the theater.

Jeeps were equipped with communications gear which allowed them to be employed in forward positions, directing air strikes and observation airplanes. With the heavy movement of refugees from the north, the military police also began to rely more on the versatile jeep. These mass movements of people brought with them infiltrators and saboteurs who had to be checked out for identity. The MPs found the jeep the perfect vehicle for this use, whether on the paved streets of cities and towns or on the dirt roads of the countryside.

Also, as in World War II, the jeep in Korea proved to be popular as a principal means of transportation for both officers and enlisted men. And again it played its customary part in many kinds of support activities, such as being converted into ambulances or used to haul supplies, equipment, and VIPs.

The M-38 jeep and the Korean Conflict appear to be living on forever in the TV show "M*A*S*H." In the early 1980s, the show in most parts of the country was still rated as one of the most popular on television. The jeep is featured or appears as a support "actor" in most of the segments. Its nightly appearance serves as a reminiscence for military personnel and for civilians as an introduction to one

To counter the problem of its being damaged by enemy fire, the rear echelons developed armor-plating for the jeep. Armor is tested in a tactical field exercise at the Kahauku training area in Hawaii in 1953.

South Korean soldiers were trained in the maintenance and working systems of the jeep so that they could become better drivers. Much use was made of Korean soldiers as drivers of American units' 4-wheel-drive vehicles, and great numbers of jeeps were assigned to Korean units.

In Korea, armor-plated windshields had to be designed and installed before the troops went on patrols.

Lt. Donald Clay of the U.S. 7th Infantry Division points to holes in the windshield of his jeep caused by Communist artillery fire near Sangyang-ni, Korea, early in the war. Sniper fire was also a problem for the jeep drivers when they got too close to the front lines.

of the roles of an important vehicle of war.

Thus, the jeep, as it is depicted in this M*A*S*H unit, is emblematic of the many ways in which it was employed in Korea during the war.

Lt. Gen. Matthew B. Ridgway, Commanding General, 8th U.S. Army, Korea (*left*); Lt. Col. Anthony F. Story, personal pilot to Gen. MacArthur; General of the Army Douglas MacArthur, Commander-in-Chief, UN Command; and Maj. Gen. F. W. Milburn, Commanding General, I Corps, touring the front lines in a jeep in March 1951.

Governor of New York Thomas E. Dewey leaves the U.S. X Corps airstrip in a jeep on his way to Hongchon at the beginning of a visit to Korea, July 9, 1951.

A convoy commander gets one of the new M-38 jeeps to lead his truck company to the front lines in Korea.

Secretary of Defense George C. Marshall departs for a tour of the front-line command posts in Korea during an inspection trip in June 1951. In the rear of the jeep are Gen. Matthew B. Ridgway (*left*), Commander-in-Chief, Far East, and Lt. Gen. James A. Van Fleet, Commanding General, 8th U.S. Army.

A typical conversion of a jeep to an ambulance. Note that the spare tire has been placed on the side. In Korea, jeeps were pressed into litter duty because there were many more wounded soldiers than usual for such a war, there were not enough ambulances to go around, and truck ambulances could not traverse the mountainous terrain.

Jeeps of the 32nd Regimental Combat Team of the 7th Infantry Division, carrying men and supplies, move up to the front lines near Umyang-ni in April 1951.

A U.S. Army jeep struck by a Chinese Communist mortar shell during the third attempt to take "Old Baldy" near Chorwon, September 20, 1952. A number of jeeps were hit by shells but, as was the case with this one, the occupants survived, basically because of the sturdy steel construction of the jeep.

Throughout the Korean Conflict, U.S. Army military police employed hundreds of jeeps in roadblocks and patrols to uncover and detect North Korean infiltrators, saboteurs, and black-marketeers. An 8th Army jeep patrol near Wonju has stopped a Korean civilian to inspect his knapsack for possible weapons or contraband.

A standard army jeep in Korea converted into an emergency vehicle fitted with fire extinguishers, medical kits, and two stretchers.

An MP safety patrol in the city of Seoul, South Korea.

Maj. Joseph E. Jenkins of the 8th Army kept the same jeep during his entire Korean tour, starting in September 1949. The jeep, "Tarheel Rebel," also experienced one combat jump. This association of jeep and soldier was sought after by the troops and was a sort of master-pet dog relationship.

A signalman of the 1st Battalion, 19th Infantry Regiment, 24th Division, lays telephone wire for communication with a Republic of Korea battalion. The 1½-ton jeep trailers saw extensive duty in Korea.

Vice-President Richard M. Nixon and President of the Republic of Korea Syngman Rhee review the troops during a parade in the IX U.S. Corps area during the vice-president's tour of Korea, November 14, 1953.

During the Korean Conflict a number of jeeps at forward combat positions were equipped with transceivers to communicate with army observation airplanes.

Many Russian-made "jeeps," copied from the U.S. lend-lease jeeps of World War II down to the smallest details, were captured from the enemy during the fighting in Korea.

The original cast of the classic "M*A*S*H" TV series mugging for a photographer on another classic, a vintage jeep M-38, veteran of the Korean Conflict.

Some of the 300 Canadian jeeps and 300 1/2-ton U.S. jeep trailers that were returned from Korea in February 1955 aboard the S.S. *Beaver State* to the port of Seattle, Washington. After the Korean Conflict ended in 1953, thousands of jeeps were declared surplus to the tactical needs of the United Nations Command and were redistributed to units throughout the world.

7 THE KAISER ERA —THE JEEP FROM 1953 TO 1969

Gen. Matthew B. Ridgway starts on his final inspection tour as the NATO commander in Europe, Basec, France, June 16, 1953.

After Kaiser Industries acquired the Willys-Overland interests in 1953, a new era unfolded for the jeep. On acquisition, the Kaiser corporation renamed the jeep operations Willys Motors, Inc. In its first two years of executive management, more than 186,000 jeeps were sold to the public. Then, in 1954, the CJ-5, an improved version of the military jeep, was put on the civilian market and it sold even better.

A year later, Kaiser reengineered the World War II military jeep for the U.S. Army, calling the new version the M-38A1. This bit of management expertise paid off handsomely, for by then the Kaiser company had nearly recouped the $60 million it had paid for the jeep operation. The M-38 jeep model was badly needed by the army to replace the World War II jeeps that were battle weary after having served in two major wars. But the M-38 came along in a period of budget cutting for the nation's military, and not all that many of the new jeeps were purchased.

In 1962, the Ford Motor Company, with the help of the army's Aberdeen Proving Ground, de-

Jeep station wagon model 685 (1953). On April 29, 1953, Willys-Overland, Inc., was acquired by the Henry J. Kaiser interests for approximately $60 million, and the name of the company was changed to Willys Motors, Inc. In the 1953 calendar year, 94,071 jeep vehicles were produced.

Jeep CJ-5 (1954). An improved civilian version of the original military jeep vehicle was introduced by Willys Motors in September 1954. In the calendar year 1954, a total of 92,165 jeep vehicles were produced in Toledo.

Willys station wagon (1955). This 2-wheel-drive jeep station wagon sported an attractive two-tone paint combination. In 1955, Willys built 12,265 station wagons.

Jeep CJ-5 (1955). Tasks previously impossible in remote off-road areas were performed with ease with the help of the incomparable Jeep Universal. Willys Motors in 1955 built 85,515 vehicles, of which 48,226 were jeep models.

An American supervisor/instructor checking the delivery of Military Defense Assistance Program jeeps to Addis Ababa, Ethiopia, in July 1956. The spare tire on this model is mounted in the front of the radiator grille, which serves as windbreaker from the blowing sand in the Ethiopian desert.

While Willys Motors was refining the civilian jeep, it was also engineering changes for the U.S. Army in the military version of the world-renowned vehicle. The M-38A1, as the new model was designated, was built until 1963, when it was superseded by the M-151.

Jeep FC-170 truck (1957). In 1957 an all-new line of forward-control trucks was announced. The FC-170 was built on a 103 5-inch wheelbase, on the same chassis as the utility wagon, and had a gross vehicle weight of 7,000 pounds. The FC-150 (*not shown*) had a wheelbase of 81 inches, on the same chassis as the CJ-5.

Working with the U.S. Army, Willys Motors in 1957 developed the unique 4-wheel-drive M-274 Mechanical Mule, which was a sort of minijeep. Powered by a 4-cylinder engine, it weighed only 750 pounds and was 100 inches long and 46 inches wide. Willys built a total of 4,618 of these units from 1957 to 1965.

veloped a redesigned jeep which they called the M-151. A 1/4-ton military utility tactical truck, it was dubbed the Mutt. The name never took, however, for the GIs still called it the jeep. The Vietnam War was on the horizon and the budgets for the army were improving each year, so the army was able to procure the M-151 model in considerable numbers. It proved to be a vastly improved model in field tests with the older M-38 jeep. Eventually it was manufactured by both Ford and Willys.

During the period from 1962 to 1969, all the branches of the U.S. military were active in putting the M-151 jeep to many different uses, both as a tactical and as a support vehicle. Fortunately again, the armed services procured the new jeep model, the M-151, in sufficient numbers to have it ready for the needs that came up for each of the services in Vietnam.

On the commercial side, the Kaiser company continued to design and manufacture new jeep lines, accompanied by a bigger advertising campaign. Other than the CJ-5 model, however, sales were not enough to bail the firm out from its losses in other areas. In February 1970, Kaiser decided to sell the jeep operation to the American Motors Corporation, which had given them the best offer. American Motors began by renaming Willys Motors the Jeep Corporation.

Jeep fire trucks (1957). Some jeep trucks were built with special fire-engine conversions, such as the FC-170 (*center*) and the CJ-2A (*front*).

In 1957, the U.S. Army awarded contracts to three American companies to design, build, and test a "flying research vehicle" that would have the versatility of the conventional jeep but also be capable of hovering and propelling itself above ground. While using the ground for protection, the "aerial jeep" would be freed from travel restrictions. The three companies failed to produce a vehicle to meet the requirements. An artist's concept of a 4-ducted propeller flying test bed of the version submitted by one of the three companies, Aerophysics Development Corporation of Santa Barbara, California.

An MP jeep being loaded aboard an Air Force C-124 cargo plane at Rhein-Main Air Force Base, Frankfurt, Germany, prior to takeoff with men and equipment for the Middle East trouble spot in Beirut, Lebanon, in July 1958.

Jeep Gala (1959). In 1959, a limited number (100) of jeep "motorized surreys with a fringe on top" were built. A fleet of them was purchased by Las Brisas Hotel in Acapulco, Mexico, each featuring a pink-and-white canvas top to complement the hotel's color motif.

The Las Brisas Hotel jeeps as they appeared twenty years later, still in perfect operating condition.

65

Jeep CJ-6 (1959). The longer-wheelbase CJ-6 had a special appeal to companies with special needs and was particularly strong in international markets.

Jeeps are also used at the Acapulco beaches to provide the tow vehicle for parachute sailing.

Jeep Harlequin (1959). Jeep stylists created this specially trimmed all-steel station wagon in 1959.

Jeep Maverick (1959). The 2-wheel-drive station wagon built in 1959 was called the Jeep Maverick. In the 1950s, Willys built vehicles called Falcon and Maverick, both of which names were later used on Ford vehicles.

Jeep CJ-5 (1960). The 1960 CJ-5 was built on an 81-inch wheelbase, one inch longer than the CJ-3B. It also was 250 pounds heavier, at 3,750 pounds. heavier, at 3,750 pounds.

Jeep Surrey (1960). The Gala became the Surrey in 1960. Two of these models were shown at the NASCAR races at Daytona International Speedway, Florida, in February.

Jeep panel delivery (1960). Many commercial establishments purchased the economical panel delivery utility vehicle that was a mainstay of the jeep line in 1960.

Jeep pickup truck (1960). Another rugged vehicle was the pickup, built on a wheelbase of 118 inches and powered by a 4- or 6-cylinder engine.

An army H-34 helicopter drops a jeep with a recoilless rifle for use by Pathfinders (advance combat troops) during a military demonstration in the Panama Canal Zone in February 1961.

Jeep CJ-5 (1961). One the many vehicles of all types built in 1961 by Willys Motors, 17,918 were CJ-3B models, 15,269 were CJ-5s, and 1,991 were CJ-6 vehicles.

A snorkel jeep leaves a landing craft during joint navy and marine amphibious Operation Greenlight at Camp Pendleton, California, in May 1961.

On the production line in the Willys plant at Toledo are the first of the M-151 1/4-ton military vehicles being built on a 1962 government contract. The all-new M-151, of single-unit construction, was built under contract by the Ford Motor Company earlier, and by AM General, an American Motors subsidiary, in the 1970s.

The individual suspension system on the army's new M-151 jeep eliminated the heavy chassis which was used on the older models.

Jeep Wagoneer (1963). In October 1962 the all-new 1963 Jeep Wagoneer was introduced. For the first time, automatic transmission was offered with a 4-wheel-drive vehicle, starting a trend toward luxury in these models. The name Willys Motors was changed in 1963 to Kaiser Jeep Corp.

Jeep Gladiator truck (1963). A line of Jeep Gladiator 4-wheel-drive trucks with gross vehicle weight ratings of 4,000 to 8,600 pounds was introduced in 1963. Built on wheelbases of 120 or 126 inches, they offered automatic transmission and other power equipment and attractive interiors. "Townside" and "Thriftside" pickup boxes and platform-stake bodies were available.

An M-151 jeep being tested at Aberdeen Proving Ground in Maryland in 1963. All models of jeeps are tested constantly to seek ways to improve them.

A machine-gun pedestal mount being tested on an M-151 jeep at Fort Knox, Kentucky, in 1963.

Below: Water wings being tested at Aberdeen, Maryland, in 1964 on an M-151 jeep. The wings are inflated by the engine exhaust gases. This device, developed by the Goodyear Aerospace Corporation, consists of easily attached flotation bags that keep the jeep waterborne while the wheels churning in the water provide propulsion.

An M-38 jeep at Fort Campbell, Kentucky, in 1964 is equipped with a 105mm recoilless rifle and has a universal helicopter sling installed.

Two soldiers admire the new M-151 jeep at Fort Sam Houston in San Antonio, Texas, one of the first camps in the 4th Army to receive the M-151 models. The new jeep was found to be faster and easier to handle due mainly to the individual suspension system on each wheel.

A World War II jeep presented to the Smithsonian Institution in Washington, D.C., for permanent display (*right*) contrasts with the modern M-151 model in use by the army at the time. The plaque on the Smithsonian jeep reads: "In tribute to its contributions as the armed forces' most versatile and useful vehicle of World War II."

Marines and sailors man an M-151 jeep equipped with a 105mm recoilless rifle at Guantanamo Bay, Cuba, on alert maneuvers in late 1963.

Every float in the inaugural parade in Washington, D.C., on January 20, 1965, for President Lyndon B. Johnson was towed by a jeep CJ-5. Several loads of the new vehicles were photographed in Toledo, Ohio.

Jeep CJ-5 Tuxedo Park (1965). In 1965, jeep stylists started a trend toward limited-edition, specially trimmed CJ models, such as the all-white Tuxedo Park. Production of all jeep vehicles in the 1965 calendar year totaled 92,366.

Jeep Super Wagoneer (1966). The popular Jeep Wagoneer 4-door station wagon received its first major styling change in 1966, including an all-new grille.

Jeep Gladiator (1966). Many 4-wheel-drive Jeep Gladiator trucks were fitted with emergency and other special equipment. Production of all jeep vehicles in calendar year 1966 totaled 74,223 units.

One of the most familiar uses for the jeep 4-wheel-drive vehicles is snowplowing. At a gasoline service station in 1966, a fleet of six jeep CJ and truck models with snowplow attachments stands ready for whatever winter may bring.

An M-151 jeep, equipped with a gas turbine and dust separator equipment, being tested at Yuma Proving Ground by the U.S. Air Force in October 1966. The tests were inconclusive.

President Lyndon B. Johnson inspects combat-ready troops of the 101st Airborne Division during his visit to Fort Campbell, Kentucky, on July 23, 1966. Riding in the jeep with the president are Maj. Gen. Ben Sternberg, commanding general of the 101st Airborne Division, and Gen. Harold K. Johnson, the army chief of staff.

Jeepster Roadster (1967). A unique body style in the new Jeepster series was this roadster with optional soft top. All Jeepsters were built on a wheelbase of 101 inches. Standard engine was the 75-hp Hurricane 4, with the 160-hp Dauntless V-6 optional. Turbo Hydra-Matic was offered with the V-6.

Jeepster station wagon (1967). With its foam-molded front buckets and rear bench seats and a wide choice of attractive trim packages, the Jeepster station wagon was the most popular body style in the new series. Production of all jeep vehicles in 1967 increased to 87,952 units.

In 1968 the army decided to adapt some of their jeeps for use in assisting in civic action riot control, particularly where National Guard units would be involved. One of the conversions was made at Fort Leonard Wood in Missouri.

Jeepster convertible model 8702 (1968). Major changes in the Jeepster convertible in 1968 included a new top, a hinged tailgate permitting ready access to cargo space behind the rear seat, full metal doors with roll-up windows, and vent wings. Jeep production in 1968 totaled 86,198 units.

Jeep "462" (1969). Special equipment on this limited-edition "462" model, based on the Jeep Universal CJ-5, included a roll bar, swing-out spare-tire carrier, Polyglas tubeless tires, skid plate, and electric ammeter and oil gauges.

Jeep Gladiator (1969). The 4-wheel-drive Jeep Gladiator truck, because of its reputation for ruggedness and dependability, was selected for slide-in camper installations by many American families. Production of all jeep vehicles in 1969 totaled 62,027.

U.S. soldiers from a psychological warfare group patrol the International Zone in the Dominican Republic in 1965, explaining to the Dominicans by loudspeakers why the United States is in the country. The army uses the M-151 jeep in many different combat-readiness roles such as this in peacetime.

8

THE JEEP IN THE VIETNAM WAR

President Lyndon B. Johnson reviews the troops at Cam Ranh Bay, Vietnam, December 23, 1967. In the center is Gen. William C. Westmoreland, commanding general of the Military Assistance Command, Vietnam, and of the United States Army, Vietnam.

A front view of an M-151 A1 jeep used at that time at Cam Ranh Bay depot by the U.S. Army as a VIP staff vehicle.

There was no shortage of jeeps in Southeast Asia in support of the Vietnam War. In fact, the employment of the jeep was more regimented in Vietnam than in the combat operations in either World War II or the Korean Conflict. In Vietnam, the army, air force, marines, navy, and Coast Guard all had jeeps in sufficient numbers.

In World War II, even though the jeep was just coming into its own, it was quickly put to use in numerous functional areas other than the planned ones. This was due to its

availability in great numbers starting in 1943. The jeep was a device to be innovative with and was jury-rigged for almost any purpose that contributed to the winning of the war.

In the Korean Conflict, the army tightened up its regulations and procedures and the innovating diminished. Unit commanders did not allow for much use of jeeps outside the intended functional areas. During the early part of the war in North Korea, the mountainous terrain somewhat restricted the jeep's

movement. But once the army was on a static line at the 38th parallel, there was more liberal utilization of the jeep. Basically, however, there were not enough jeeps in Korea to allow for other than combat use.

In Vietnam, the jeep was available in sufficient numbers in the units, and because of the restrictions of the troops to enclaves, it was available for many forms of transportation. Its role was far-reaching throughout Southeast Asia in support of the Vietnam War, though mainly within the confines

Adm. David L. McDonald, chief of naval operations, acompanied by Lt. Gen. Lewis W. Walt, U.S. Marine Corps, inspects the troops from a jeep while on an inspection visit to Danang, Vietnam, in November 1966.

Officers of the 1st Cavalry Division (Airmobile) hold a last-minute briefing and lunch over a jeep hood before moving out in a sweep against the enemy during Operation Masher in 1966.

Early in the Vietnam War it was believed that because it was to be a war of skirmishes, the jeep could not venture throughout the combat areas without armor plating for its occupants. Therefore, lightweight armor plating was developed for protection in ambush attacks. As it turned out, the war developed differently and this innovation was not developed further.

of the intended uses. Indeed, the military employed the jeep very efficiently.

The procurement of the M-151 model in 1962 by the army gave its units time to test the new design and determine the various roles—tactical and support—that it would serve. Jeeps became an item of issue to units according to their table of distribution. Therefore, when a division deployed to Vietnam, its units carried jeeps right along with them, just as an infantryman carried his own rifle.

For the first time, the jeep could be outfitted with the M-60 .50-caliber machine gun and the 106mm recoilless rifle as standard operating equipment. This better-planned use of the jeep increased its popularity among the younger soldiers, sailors, marines, and airmen. They were won over to the jeep in the same way their fathers and older brothers had been in two earlier wars. Probably the best evaluation of the jeep in Vietnam came from one of the commanding generals of the Military Assistance Command, Vietnam, Gen. Creighton W. Abrams, who said, "The jeep was the primary vehicle of the Vietnam War."

Once they were in Vietnam, the jeeps were often transferred by air. An army sergeant claims his jeep and drives it out the back of an army C-7 Caribou. It had been requested to support a military operation near Duc Lap in 1966.

A jeep of the 17th Cavalry Regiment, mounting an M-60 .50-caliber machine gun, helps secure a landing zone for a wave of UH-1D helicopters carrying members of the 31st Infantry Division during Operation Junction City, Phase II near Tay Ninh City in 1967. During the Vietnam War, jeeps were regularly used to secure landing-and-search operations.

Troop E of the 17th Cavalry Division's 173rd Airborne Battalion is deployed and in action with its jeeps along an enemy-held public road during highway-securing operations near landing zone "English" in February 1969. The jeeps are equipped with both the 106mm recoilless rifle and the M-60 machine gun.

Comedian Danny Kaye rides in a jeep from the heliport to his United Services Organization appearance in a visit to Cu Chi during the Vietnam War in April 1966. Maj. Gen. Fred C. Weyand, the 25th Infantry Division commander, is riding in the "hump" seat in back.

Members of the 4th Battalion, 39th Infantry, 9th Infantry Division, utilize the hood of a jeep as a field pharmacy during a "Medcap" operation that was to administer to the emergency medical needs of the Vietnamese populace in their area. Hundreds of jeeps were used throughout Vietnam for this type of civic action in the communities.

A sweep is finished and a jeep prepares to pull out and return to base camp with its fully laden trailer as part of Operation Junction City, Phase II, 1967.

During Operation Pershing, jeeps with radios and M-60 machine guns were used along Route 1 to relay orders to advancing troops and to stand guard against Vietcong attacks.

Officers of the 82nd Airborne Division use the hood of a jeep as a command-post table while coordinating troop positions in their encampment at Phu Bai, Vietnam, in 1968.

U.S. marine jeeps, both M-38 and M-151, in line prior to being loaded on board a C-141 cargo plane deploying the 5th Marine Division to Vietnam in February 1968.

The jeep was used extensively by commanders in the field as command posts from which to dispense orders. The commander of the 3rd Battalion of the 82nd Division gives his executive officer final instructions before driving to the staging area to begin combat operations, in 1968.

As in World War II and the Korean Conflict, in the Vietnam War the jeep had high priority with all personnel right down to the company clerk. Every unit headquarters had its contingent of jeeps parked outside. A unit with the 5th Infantry Division, Mechanized, at Quang Tri in 1968.

Gen. William C. Westmoreland, commanding general of the Military Assistance Command, Vietnam, and Korea's minister of national defense, Sung Eun Kim, prepare to troop the line at Kimpo International Airport, Seoul, following the general's arrival for a visit to Korea.

The M-151 jeep saw all kinds of duty in Vietnam. Two MACV (Military Assistance Command, Vietnam) military police jeeps escort a U.S. Navy vehicle carrying a payroll from one of the navy compounds in Cholon, a suburb of Saigon.

Gen. Creighton W. Abrams, commanding general of MACV in the latter years of the war, was an admirer of the jeep and used it constantly. In June 1969, he troops the lines of the 25th Infantry Division at Cu Chi, Vietnam.

The need for jeeps in Vietnam was so great that vehicles damaged in accidents sometimes had to be airlifted to a repair depot—often the only means of getting there. A CH-47 Chinook helicopter of the 101st Airborne Division airlifts a jeep from the base at Mai Loc to Camp Evans for repair.

Vietnamese medics put a wounded soldier from the 23rd ARVN (Army Republic of Vietnam) Division into a hospital jeep to transport him to a medical facility at Ban Me Thout.

All of the Republic of Vietnam services made extensive use of the jeep. The plentiful rains and resultant mud made constant maintenance necessary to keep the vehicles as clean as possible. Quang Tri, December 1969.

Because most of the Vietnamese traffic on the roads consisted of bicycles and motor bikes, the jeep was the perfect vehicle to ride herd on them to check the identification of the riders and weed out the enemy. Near the U.S. Army encampment at Binh Dinh, an MP checks the ID (identification) of local civilians.

An air force mobile air-traffic-control team directs a C-123 to a safe landing on a small airstrip at Dau Tieng, using a communications-rigged jeep. Jeeps were used throughout Vietnam as mobile "control towers" for air operations.

The U.S. Air Force made extensive use of the jeep in Vietnam, utilizing thousands of them from their inventories worldwide. An air force sergeant at Cam Ranh Bay air base, a huge aerial and sea port, records C-7 Caribou resupply sorties in support of the Republic of Vietnam Army.

The jeep played a popular role in liaison missions involving troops of other nations. At Phu Cat air base two air force officers (*left*) are in the beginning steps of an air-strike exercise with a Korean army officer (*right*).

One of the most far-reaching users of the jeeps in the army in Vietnam was the military police, particularly in the forward combat zones with miscellaneous duties including filtering out the Vietcong from the general populace that was always on the roads. Brig. Gen. Wallace K. Wittwer, commanding officer of the 18th MP Brigade (*right*), is briefed on the situation shortly after arriving at an advance combat position at Khe San.

A chaplain of the 101st Airborne Division in Vietnam is saying Mass and starting to serve communion using the hood of a jeep as an altar, as many chaplains did before him in the two previous U.S. wars.

9 AMERICAN MOTORS TAKES CONTROL —THE JEEP SINCE 1970

Early in 1970 the American Motors Corporation purchased the Jeep Company from Kaiser Industries and renamed it the Jeep Corporation. This was the beginning of a new concept in manufacturing and merchandising for the jeep vehicles. American Motors started introducing new commercial models in 1971 and concentrated on developing a number of civilian jeeps patterned after the ruggedness of the military vehicle. In quick succession, they brought out the Cherokee and Renegade in 1974, the Cherokee Chief in 1975, and the Honcho in 1976. Since then they have added the Laredo and Scrambler, both in keeping with the new popular "macho" theme. All of these versions of the jeep have been well received by the public.

The jeep advertising campaigns of American Motors have also stressed the theme of ruggedness. Specially placed ads in such magazines as *Playboy* and *Sports Afield* reached people of all ages who were seeking a macho image.

Since the end of the Vietnam War the military have been doing considerable planning. They were very

Jeep Gladiator truck (1970). The Jeep Gladiator truck for 1970 featured a new grille and optional two-tone paint combinations. In February 1970, Kaiser Jeep was purchased from Kaiser Industries by American Motors and renamed Jeep Corporation. The new company immediately began a program to upgrade the jeep product line.

In 1970, Jeep Corporation stylists created the XJ001, a fresh design concept in 4-wheel-drive vehicles. Built on a Jeep Universal CJ-5 chassis, the one-of-a-kind "idea" prototype had an 81-inch wheelbase, extra-wide tread, and plastic body.

pleased with the increased firepower of the 106mm recoilless rifle on the M-151 jeep. Next, the "TOW" antitank missile made its appearance on the M-151, and the army and marines both liked its performance in tests and training. But there is a concern as to whether the basic weight of the jeep is equal to handling the increased weight loads being deployed on it by automotive engineers who want the jeep to be more than a jeep.

With the jeep being modified with heavier and heavier armament, the army has decided it needs a big brother to the jeep—a diesel-powered, automatic-transmissioned vehicle that can carry a 2,500-pound load and have a cruising range of 300 miles. AM General, a subsidiary of the American Motors Corporation, and two other manufacturers, Teledyne and Chrysler, have built twelve models each to meet the army's requirements. The vehicles will be tested and studied over a long period of time, and then a contract will be awarded to the winner, in what appears to be the same sort of procurement process that the jeep went through in 1940.

After World War II there were many conversions of wartime American jeeps around the world. The most lasting (to this day) was in the Philippines, where an estimated 10,000 of the vehicles found their way into transportation as "jeepneys" or taxis. In its basic form the Jeepney had an extended rear platform, seated about twelve people, and had an entrance from the rear. In about 1970 there were still some 5,000 of these gaily decorated World War II Jeeps in service as taxis throughout the Philippine Islands. By then, the demand outstripped their availability from the various Pacific islands where they had been abandoned by the U.S. Government, and inflation allowed the taxi drivers to buy substitute, near-facsimile "jeeps" from Western Europe and Japan.

A U.S. Army mobile satellite-communications field station, erected on a jeep platform, in service at Sinsheim, West Germany, during the NATO exercise Reforger II in October 1970. The mobile field station is able to communicate with the continental United States via a satellite-communications link-up.

Hurst/Jeepster Special (1971). A customized Jeepster Commando station wagon built in limited numbers was the Hurst/Jeepster Special, which featured rally stripes on the cowl and tailgate, wide-tread tires, scoop-mounted tachometer, and a choice of Hurst's Dual Gate shifter with automatic transmission or T-handle shifter with manual.

Jeep Wagoneer (1971). Early in 1971 the American Motors 304 CID and 360 CID V-8 engines became options in the Wagoneer and in Gladiator truck models, with the AMC 258 CID 6 standard. The General Products Division, formed to concentrate on defense and special products, was established in March as AM General Corp., an AMC subsidiary. The 1960 CJ-5 model was modernized to become the main vehicle sold to the U.S. Postal Service.

Actually, the army is not seeking a replacement for the jeep but rather a replacement for three vehicles—the 1/4-ton jeep, the 1/2-ton truck, and the 1 1/4-ton Gamma Goat. The new vehicle, dubbed the HMMWV (High-Mobility, Multipurpose wheeled vehicle), or Hummer, will solve many of the army's tactical problems. The army hopes to have the Hummer in the field ready for combat by 1984. But in the end the military jeep will perhaps prove to be irreplaceable.

An army M-151 jeep being dropped by a U.S. Army UH-1 helicopter as part of support equipment for the XM-204 soft-recoil 105mm howitzer during a Bold Shot 4-71 exercise at Fort Bragg, North Carolina, in the spring of 1971.

Jeep Renegade II (1971). The limited-edition Jeep Renegade II was shown for the first time at the Detroit Auto Show early in 1971. It featured as standard equipment many custom-performance items including special striping, roll bar, and tachometer. Jeep production in 1971 increased to 53,480 units.

Jeep Commando station wagon (1972). The Jeepster Commando became the Commando in 1972 and was introduced with an all-new front-end design. Beginning in 1972, all jeep vehicles were powered by American Motors engines, with V-8s available throughout the line for the first time.

The U.S. Army Tank Automotive Command at Warren, Michigan, in May 1972 demonstrated the development of a run-flat folding sidewall tire which, when used in combat conditions, allowed the jeep to be driven up to 60 miles without requiring the driver to stop and change the tire or abandon the vehicle.

Jeep Wagoneer (1973). A revolutionary, full-time, 4-wheel-drive system, Quadra-Trac, was introduced on the Jeep Wagoneer and on four Jeep truck models in 1973, adding significant new benefits in mobility and safety.

Jeep truck (1973). Introduced at the 1973 Chicago Auto Show was a truck model with a special cap, an aluminum cab-height cover with side and rear windows. Production of jeep vehicles continued to climb in 1973, totaling 94,035 for the year.

Jeep Cherokee (1974). New in 1974 was the Jeep Cherokee 2-door sports/utility vehicle, built on a wheelbase of 109 inches. Its many unique features accented its appeal to recreational-vehicle buyers. The Commando series was dropped in 1974.

Jeep Wagoneer (1974). The 1974 Jeep Wagoneer, sporting a new front-end design, became the industry's most completely equipped 4-wheel-drive sports/utility vehicle. Standard on all models were Quadra-Trac full-time 4WD, 360 CID V-8 engine, automatic transmission, power steering, and front power-disc brakes.

Jeep Renegade (1974). Previously available on a limited basis, the sporty Jeep CJ-5 Renegade became a regular production model in 1974. Powered by the American Motors 304 CID V-8, it featured special paint treatment, rear-mounted spare tire, roll bar, passenger safety rail, dual sun visors, oil and amp gauges, and forged-aluminum-styled wheels.

Jeep truck (1974). Quadra-Trac full-time 4WD was made available on the complete jeep truck line in 1974, with both 6- and 8-cylinder engines. All trucks featured bigger brakes and shorter turning diameter. Jeep production in the 1974 calendar year reached 96,645 vehicles.

An M-151 jeep is used by U.S. navy Seabees in 1974 in building the Dublon Road in the Truk District of the Trust Territory of the Pacific Islands.

Jeep Wagoneer (1975). Among many improvements made in the 1975 Jeep Wagoneer were an optional new wood-grain side-panel treatment, electronic ignition system, new power-steering gear, and new shocks and springs.

The U.S. Navy as well as the U.S. Army made extensive use of the M-151 jeep throughout the world in the 1970s. Lt. James MacLaughlin, commanding officer of Navy Construction Battalion Maintenance Unit 302, prepares to depart on his daily duties at the naval station at Subic Bay, Republic of the Philippines, July 21, 1975.

Jeep Cherokee Chief (1975). Shown first at the Detroit Auto Show in January 1975 was the sporty Cherokee Chief model, which featured extra-wide track and chassis components, wide tires, and many other distinctive trim touches.

Jeep CJ-7 (1976). In 1976, Jeep Corp. introduced the all-new CJ-7 model with optional one-piece removable hardtop, automatic transmission, and Quadra-Trac drive. Built on a wheelbase of 93.5 inches, the CJ-7 hardtop was offered with steel side doors and liftgate. An optional soft top also was available.

Jeep Wagoneer (1976). All 1976 jeep models featured new, more rugged frames and a wide range of design and mechanical improvements.

Jeep truck (1976). Three truck models were included in the 1976 jeep line. In the J-10 series, two models with wheelbases of 119 and 131 inches were offered. One model in the J-20 series was built on a 131-inch wheelbase.

97

Jeep Cherokee Chief (1976). The Cherokee Chief proved so popular following its introduction on a limited scale in 1975 that it was made a full-fledged member of the jeep family in 1976. Standard equipment included power-disc brakes, power steering, and fuel-tank skid plate.

At the U.S. Naval Academy, Annapolis, Maryland, in 1977, Richard Blaser sits in the driver's seat of NAHBE I. An old army M-151 jeep, it is powered by a heat-balanced engine modified by Blaser and his associate engineer, Dr. Andrew Pouring, during experiments at the academy. The engine achieves more efficient combustion through the addition of mushroom-shaped caps machined to the tops of the pistons along with a modified air/fuel intake system.

Jeep Cherokee 4-door (1977). In 1977, Jeep Corp. added a 4-door model to the popular Cherokee series. A 2-barrel 258 CID 6-cylinder engine and front power-disc brakes were made standard in all Cherokee models.

Jeep CJ-7 (1977). Many refinements were made in the CJ-5 and CJ-7 for 1977, including frames with full box-section side rails and strengthened rear-body panels.

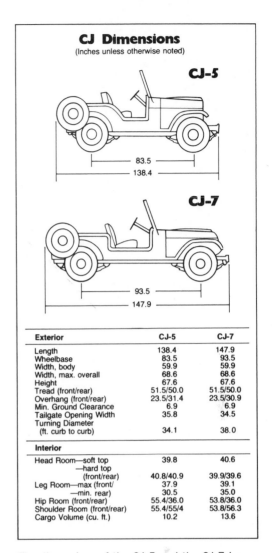

CJ Dimensions
(Inches unless otherwise noted)

CJ-5
83.5
138.4

CJ-7
93.5
147.9

Exterior	CJ-5	CJ-7
Length	138.4	147.9
Wheelbase	83.5	93.5
Width, body	59.9	59.9
Width, max. overall	68.6	68.6
Height	67.6	67.6
Tread (front/rear)	51.5/50.0	51.5/50.0
Overhang (front/rear)	23.5/31.4	23.5/30.9
Min. Ground Clearance	6.9	6.9
Tailgate Opening Width	35.8	34.5
Turning Diameter (ft. curb to curb)	34.1	38.0
Interior		
Head Room—soft top	39.8	40.6
—hard top (front/rear)	40.8/40.9	39.9/39.6
Leg Room—max (front/	37.9	39.1
—min. rear)	30.5	35.0
Hip Room (front/rear)	55.4/36.0	53.8/36.0
Shoulder Room (front/rear)	55.4/55/4	53.8/56.3
Cargo Volume (cu. ft.)	10.2	13.6

The dimensions of the CJ-5 and the CJ-7 jeeps.

Jeep Cherokee 2-door (1977). Cherokee 2-door models for 1977 included a base model and the wide-track version with newly styled steel wheels and raised white-letter tires, plus wider axles and flared front- and rear-wheel openings.

Jeep CJ-5 (1977). Front disc brakes, manual or power, replaced power drum brakes as options for all CJ models in 1977. To acommodate the disc brakes, as well as new optional wide wheels and tires, the front axle was upgraded, including stronger wheel spindles.

Jeep truck (1977). Gross vehicle weight ratings for 1977 jeep 4-wheel-drive trucks were boosted for increased payloads. The standard rating of 6,500 pounds was increased to 6,800 pounds while the optional 7,200- and 8,000-pound ratings were increased by 400 pounds each.

Jeep Honcho (1977). The distinctive Honcho package continued in 1977 as an option on the J-10 truck with 119-inch wheelbase. A blue Levi's fabric bench seat and Levi's inserts in door panels were some of the special features.

In 1978, M-151 jeeps of the U.S. Marines are staged on the starboard elevator on call as the marines conduct a helicopter assault from the amphibious assault ship USS *Guadalcanal* during Operation Solid Shield. Note the "TOW" antitank missile equipment mounted on the jeeps.

100

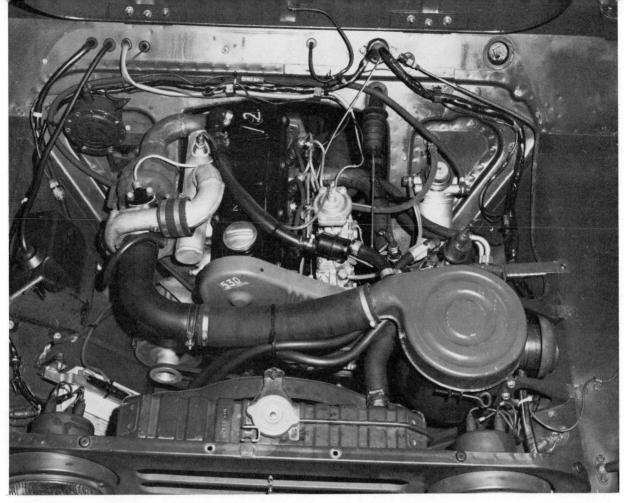

The A2 model version of the M-151, which made its appearance in early 1978, shows that under the hood it has the most compacted engine area of any jeep to date.

The newly designed jeep trailer, the M-416, made its debut in March 1978.

The jeep-mounted 106mm (M-40) rifles, which first saw action in the Vietnam War, became a mainstay of the jeeps in combat units. The 1st Battalion of the 178th CBS at Fort McCoy, Wisconsin, practices on the firing range with the big guns in July 1978.

June 27, 1978, was a banner day in jeep history, marking the highest annual level of production ever achieved when the 150,000th jeep rolled off the assembly line at the old Willys plant in Toledo, Ohio. Ohio governor James A. Rhodes was there to drive the record-breaking Jeep Renegade off the production line. Seated next to him was the then president of American Motors, Gerald C. Meyers.

Comedian Redd Foxx, an avid racer, drives his CJ-7 with two wheels in the air.

And with all four wheels off the track after a mishap, he and his partner crawl out of their jeep unhurt.

Actress Elke Sommer at the start of the 1978 Las Vegas celebrity race.

Jeeps have been entered in many auto races and events over the years and have been winners. The most interesting event to date must be the Jeep Celebrity Challenge Race held on June 25, 1978, in Las Vegas, Nevada. The winning team consisted of James Brolin, who played Dr. Kiley on the successful "Marcus Welby, M.D." TV show, and Grant Randall, owner of Randall AMC/Jeep of Mesa, Arizona. They put their trophy to good use.

1978 heralded few if any changes in the jeep line of vehicles. However, an optional package was available on the CJ-5 and CJ-7: the Golden Eagle. It included an eagle visual and name decal on the hood of the vehicle, plus golden wheels and striping.

The biggest news of 1979 was the unprecedented success of the Jeep Wagoneer Limited. This top-of-the-line Wagoneer had all the most-wanted options as standard equipment. A luxurious interior was highlighted by wood-grain detailing, automatic windows, and extra-quiet insulation.

Pete Rose, star of the Cincinnati Reds baseball team, upon leaving the club in 1979 bought ten Jeep CJs and gave nine of them to members of the team, including coaches and the trainer. Rose sits on the hood of the tenth jeep, a CJ-7 which he kept for himself. The baseball player had his first love affair with the jeep when he received one in 1975 after winning the Most Valuable Player Award in the World Series that year.

1980 signaled the turn toward economy. The entire jeep lineup benefited from improvements in gas mileage. A new 4-cylinder, 2.5 liter Hurricane engine became available in the CJ line to deliver the best mileage yet in the sports/utility category.

Bright Star '82, the largest test ever conducted by the U.S. Rapid Deployment Force, used jeeps of the 82nd Combat Aviation Battalion very successfully in the Egyptian desert in the joint military exercise. The U.S. soldiers can be seen wearing sand masks and glasses.

President Ronald W. Reagan in his CJ-6 jeep at his ranch in southern California.

After the huge success of packages like the Renegade and Golden Eagle, Jeep added the Laredo package. Available on CJs and Cherokees, the Laredo featured unique chrome accents, striping, and tinted windows.

Jeep Corporation's line of Cherokee and Wagoneer models expanded for 1981 with a 4-door model available on Cherokees, including the sporty Cherokee Chief, and a Brougham added to the successful Wagoneer line.

In 1980 the Philippine Government issued two commemorative postage stamps to honor the American World War II jeep turned "jeepney."

The American Motors entry in the U.S. military's high-mobility, multipurpose wheeled-vehicle competition is nicknamed the Hummer. It is one of three vehicles being considered from Teledyne, General Dynamics, and American Motors General.

At the end of World War II, Willys-Overland Motors of Toledo, Ohio, undertook the manufacture of private and commercial versions of the jeep. The first "civilian jeep" was designated the CJ-2 Universal. It was in most respects very similar to the military jeep, except that it had a mounted spare tire and a tailgate. Little or no advertising supported this first peacetime 4-wheeler. In spite of a lack of advertising support, the CJ-2 sold 3,200 units in its introductory year. Clearly there was something uniquely appealing about the jeep to a peacetime America. There was hardly a single former military person who did not yearn to own a version of the jeep as a private automobile.

The jeep name signaled a warmly accepted friend with a reputation for dependability and courage earned in combat. And jeep vehicles, because of their 4-wheel-drive system, offered capabilities to the public beyond simple transportation. Beyond that, there was mystique about the jeep: it was manly, or, to use a more recent term, macho. This association resulted in big sales for the civilian jeep vehicles. It might be difficult for a psychiatrist to explain the emotional appeal, but it was there.

The 1942 ad for Willys-Overland captured the spirit of the jeep and the emotions of a nation. This "Mustang of Metal" was the symbol of a young and energetic America ready to do battle and get the messy business of war over with once and for all.

The Sun Never Sets On the Mighty "Jeep"

VIVE LES AMERICAINS! VIVE LA FRANCE! VIVE LE JEEP!

A WORD PICTURE OF THE HOUR OF LIBERATION IN ORLEANS, 1944

ON THE morning of August 17th, 1944, Nazi-infested Orleans came suddenly alive. The air was charged with suppressed excitement. Emotions were masked, but French hearts beat wildly. For the glorious news was being flashed from lip to ear, that the victorious Americans were marching toward the city. Liberation was at hand.

All that day and night the air trembled from the violence of the fighting. Next morning a joyful, almost hysterical Orleans realized that the hated Nazis had fled.

Soon the welcome roar of American motors was heard, and the people streamed forth from their homes and shops.

Some hastened toward the oncoming Americans. Others gathered round the statue of Joan of Arc.

Into the city and straight to the square the first

In the center of the city square in Orleans, looking out over the gleaming river Loire, there stands a statue of Joan of Arc, the saint-like peasant maiden who in 1429, led an awed and inspired army against the enemies of France, raised the critical siege of Orleans, and saved France for Frenchmen. Today her name is hallowed throughout all of France as a saint and the immortal liberator.

Americans came—strong, forthright young fighting men with friendly grins on their battle-stained faces. For a few seconds the deep emotions of the people held their lips silent. Then a single clarion

voice pierced the stillness—"Vive le Jeep," it cried. And the crowd, their suppressed emotions suddenly released, shouted, cried, wept and joined the chorus—"Vive Les Americains! Vive la France! Vive le Jeep."

And so, in the shadow of the statue of their saintly liberator, Joan of Arc, the overjoyed people of Orleans gave thanks to a modern deliverer who came, not on a prancing white horse, but in steeds of steel called "Jeeps."

★ ★ ★

In France and in every country in the world, the mighty "Jeep" is a symbol of freedom and of American genius—clean, rugged, tough and dependable! A mighty servant in war—and a mighty servant for the coming dawn of a golden era of peace. Willys-Overland Motors, Inc., Toledo 1, Ohio.

Willys *Builds the Mighty* 'Jeep'

Victory! And Willys Jeep celebrates as all good soldiers do. This ad running in late 1944 pays tribute to the men and machines that helped turn the tide. The small motor car from Toledo, Ohio, has truly become an international household word.

Encouraged by their initial success, Willys-Overland elected to enter the automobile marketplace on a larger scale. It was clear that to accomplish this, they would have to advertise.

In the 1948 and 1949 model years, two new entries were offered. The first was the model 4-63, a 2-door, metal-sided station wagon, which was offered in 2-wheel drive only. (In 1950, the 4-63 was offered in both 2-wheel and 4-wheel drive.) The second was the sporty model VJ-2 or Jeepster, which was offered with a choice of 4-cylinder or 6-cylinder L-head engine. The Jeepster came with a folding canvas top and clear plastic snap-down rear and side windows. All were 2-wheel drive, and boasted of sporty good fun, as was shown in a 1950 ad that ran in *National Geographic* magazine.

In 1953, the year the Henry J. Kaiser Industries bought out the Willys assets and named their newly acquired subsidiary Willys Motors, Inc., the CJ-3B was introduced. Its advertising was mostly confined to farm journals and construction-industry trade publications. The CJ-3B offered several improvements over its predecessor, including one-piece windshield glass, a gas filler access outside of the vehicle, and a 6-cylinder, 250-horsepower V engine option. The vehicle still had the Willys name stamped on the side and rear tailgate.

In 1955, two new jeep vehicles were introduced, the CJ-5 and the CJ-6. The CJ-5 was the forerunner of the jeep vehicles sold today. The Willys name on the side and rear finally came off with this model. The CJ-5 had an 81-inch wheelbase. The CJ-6 was a stretch model of the CJ-5 with a 101-inch wheelbase. Both of these vehicles were marketed primarily to the farm and construction industries. The CJ-6 was also aggressively marketed for export purposes; the side-mounted fold-down seat configuration in the rear could comfortably carry eight people and equipment, making it an ideal vehicle for military uses.

In the same year, the DJ-3A Dispatcher was introduced. This vehicle, available only in 2-wheel drive, was advertised primarily for commercial fleets and for U.S. Postal Service use. Produced by Kaiser, the DJ-3A was an enclosed vehicle. The hard metal cab had sliding side doors and a rear side-opening door. Many of these models were built with a right-hand drive configuration to suit the requirements of rural postal delivery.

(cont'd on p. 118)

The CJ-2 Universal Jeep introduced in 1946, at a retail price of approximately $1,600.

You've never owned a car so useful, so practical

NO sedan can match a station wagon for all-around usefulness. And no other station wagon is so practical for every use as the "Jeep" Station Wagon—the first with an all-steel body and top for greater safety and longer service. It's a roomy, comfortable family car. When you need extra big load space, all except the driver's seat are removable. Let your Willys-Overland dealer show you how fully the "Jeep" Station Wagon meets your family's needs.

LOTS OF ROOM inside the "Jeep" Station Wagon's all-steel body for passengers—space, too, for things you want to take along. When there's a bulky load to haul, such as a chair or washing machine to be repaired, removing the seats gives 96 cubic feet of cargo space.

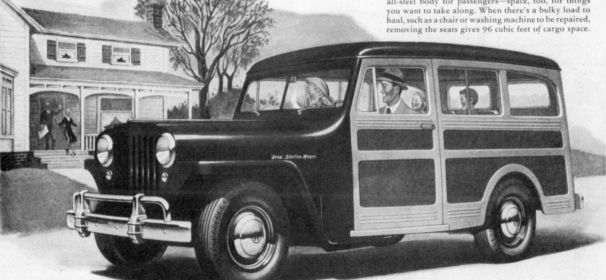

WONDERFULLY SMOOTH RIDING on country roads as well as city streets. Independent front-wheel suspension absorbs road bumps, keeping the car level and steady. It's a thrifty car to drive—the world-famous "Jeep" Engine with overdrive delivers mileage to brag about.

LET IT SNOW or rain or the sun beat down—the "Jeep" Station Wagon's all-steel body and top can take it. Even more important, you drive a "Jeep" Station Wagon with the secure feeling of sturdy steel around and above you.

'Jeep' Station Wagon
WITH STEEL BODY AND TOP

 WILLYS-OVERLAND MOTORS, TOLEDO
MAKERS OF AMERICA'S MOST USEFUL VEHICLES

The model 463, a 2-door metal-sided station wagon, was introduced in 1946 in 2-wheel drive only. Two years later it became available in both 2- and 4-wheel drive.

THE POWER, maneuverability and speed of the Universal "Jeep" make it a perfect service vehicle for garages, filling stations and fleet owners. Truck bed hauls supplies and tools.

4-WHEEL-DRIVE TRACTION takes the "Jeep" cross-country and through mud, snow and sand. When men and tools *must* get there, you know you can depend on a "Jeep", despite roads and weather.

IF YOU HAVE TOUGH JOBS, AND LOTS OF THEM
GET A 'Jeep'

COMING
—Surprise of the year from Willys-Overland . . . a new way to use "Jeep" power. Watch for announcement soon.

Business after business is discovering two advantages of the Universal "Jeep" that set it apart from other vehicles, that make it a cost-cutting investment—

1. "JEEP" PERFORMANCE: The economical power of the Willys-Overland "Jeep" Engine. Maneuverability and short turning radius. Selective 2- and 4-wheel drive, giving 6 speeds forward, 2 reverse; operating range of 2 to 60 mph; traction for heavy pulling and cross-country travel.

2. "JEEP" VERSATILITY: Serves as pick-up or tow truck . . . as a personnel carrier . . . as a plant-yard or field tractor . . . as a mobile power unit for belt- and shaft-driven equipment.

Ask a Willys-Overland dealer to demonstrate the Universal "Jeep's" ability to handle your tough jobs.

Willys-Overland Motors, Inc. • Toledo 1, Ohio

MOBILE ARC-WELDING SERVICE anywhere, any time, with the "Jeep" equipped with this 200 amp. arc-welding unit, with generator operated by V-belt drive from power take-off. Ask your dealer about it.

USED AS A LIGHT TRACTOR, the "Jeep" pulls gang-mowers at airports or clubs . . . tows trailers . . . operates most farm implements. Rear power take-off runs equipment driven by spline-shaft or pulley.

wherever there's fun, there you will find the people

this car was made for . . . people with a flair for the unusual;

who combine smartness, unerring good taste *and* a sharp sense of value

it's the Jeepster

There's a challenge in the Jeepster. You feel an invitation to get-in-and-go that is unmatched in any other American-built car. Try sitting, low and relaxed, in the driver's seat. You'll know you're in the most exciting thing on four wheels in all motordom. Try to resist the urge to roam the roads and skim along the boulevards . . . with the Jeepster as your companion.

There's a singing joyful way about this car. There's also a lack of dead weight . . . an absence of stale ideas in automotive design. The Jeepster is refreshing and new and *fun.*

The only thing like it is another Jeepster. And this year, many people like you are going to make that happy discovery.

Meet the Jeepster now at Willys-Overland dealers.

WILLYS-OVERLAND MOTORS, TOLEDO, OHIO, U.S.A. • MAKERS OF AMERICA'S MOST USEFUL VEHICLES

113

A sporty 2-wheel-drive version of the trusty jeep, the VJ-2 Jeepster, was introduced in 1950. This ad ran in *National Geographic*, a magazine that was obviously expected to reach the adventurous outdoor type. The Jeepster represented the first recognition of the recreational potential of Jeep-brand vehicles.

With the CJ-3B in 1953, innovations, however small, began to upgrade the workmanlike jeep for the American consumer. One-piece window glass replaced the dual-glass windshield, and the gas filler cap was relocated outside the vehicle instead of beneath the driver's seat. The famous 250-hp V-6 Hurricane engine was also introduced as an option. The Willys name was stamped prominently into the side and the tailgate.

The CJ-5 Universal (1955). A higher, rounded hood to enclose a larger engine and rounded fenders were the most striking differences of this jeep vehicle. It had a side-mounted spare and was the first CJ with a 12-volt electrical system. It sold for approximately $1,685.

The CJ-6 (1955) was a stretch version of the CJ-5. Twenty inches of longer wheelbase cut down on the maneuverability of this 4-wheelbase but greatly enhanced its load capacity. Twin side-mounted benches in the rear allowed the vehicle to carry eight people with ease, and ideal military configuration. Indeed, many armies around the world are making use of the CJ-6 today.

The DJ-3A Dispatcher, a 2-wheel-drive minivan, made an ideal commercial vehicle. Introduced in 1955, it was the forerunner of the DJ-5, which became the mainstay delivery vehicle of the U.S. Postal Service.

The 'Jeep' Wagoneer with 4-wheel drive has twice the traction of ordinary station wagons.

Let the other guy worry...you go in snow!

Ever wondered nervously if you would make it home through a heavy snowstorm that the weather bureau predicted would only be "flurries"?

Worry no more. When everyone else comes to a stop, you go in your new 'Jeep' Wagoneer with 4-wheel drive. That's because it has twice the traction of con-ventional station wagons. It goes where no ordinary station wagon ever could!

Pull one simple lever and you're in 4-wheel drive. Up mountains, around slippery corners, through snow, mud and sand, the 'Jeep' Wagoneer gets you through. It has easy riding comfort, plus the largest load space of any wagon in its field. And it comes with a full range of options like automatic transmission, power steering and power brakes.

Discover what confidence the new 'Jeep' Wagoneer can add to your driving. Stop in at your 'Jeep' dealer and test drive one of the "Unstoppables."

KAISER **Jeep** *CORPORATION*
TOLEDO 1, OHIO
KAISER 50 YEARS

First really new family wagon in years. 'Jeep' Wagoneer with 4-wheel drive.

See 'Jeep' vehicles in action on TV..."CBS Evening News With Walter Cronkite."

The 1962 Jeep Wagoneer, with 4-wheel drive, had twice the traction of ordinary station wagons, even in conditions of intense snow. The Wagoneer was successfully advertised as the "first really new family wagon in years."

Look what's happened to the original 'Jeep' work-and-hobby horse.

Here's where you leave other sports cars behind!

There's just no stopping the new Tuxedo Park Mark IV. It's the smart way to go sporting. With 'Jeep' 4-wheel drive you have an edge on the crowd. Take it down to the beach—up on the ski trail—out in the boondocks. It's part of the fun!

Just pull one simple lever and you're in 4-wheel drive. Ready to go off-the-road ...or up those slippery hills in town. It goes where others can't.

It's the new idea in sports cars with its smart new color combinations and bright trim. It's a <u>real</u> sports car. Take it to the golf club or to your cabana. It's welcome wherever people are out for fun.

Join the "Unstoppables." Available in two sizes: 81 inch and 101 inch wheelbases. Choice of colorful convertible tops. Test drive a Tuxedo Park Mark IV at your 'Jeep' dealer's soon.

KAISER Jeep CORPORATION
TOLEDO 1, OHIO

New idea in sports cars. 'Jeep' Tuxedo Park Mark IV with 4-wheel drive.

Advertising for the CJ-5A, Tuxedo Park, stressed that when the workday is over, this work horse becomes a "new idea in sports cars." The supersporty CJ-5A, introduced in 1965, retailed for approximately $1,900.

Actor Danny Thomas was featured in a 1967 advertising campaign for the Jeepster. The slogan: "Holy Toledo, what a car!" The Jeepster retailed for approximately $2,600.

For ten years, no changes were made in the short-wheelbase civilian jeep vehicles. Improvements in interior appointments and safety upgrading of lights, glass, and tires were the main areas concentrated on.

Year after year, as the Model 463 jeep 2-door station wagon continued to sell well, use of advertising increased. Attempts were made to market other jeep models, but it was not until Kaiser introduced the Jeep Wagoneer in 1962 that they found a model that outsold the station wagon. By 1962, the veteran of World War II was beginning to prosper and build a family. Kaiser now looked for a way to serve this consumer and found it in a semiluxury car that still possessed an element of ruggedness. The Wagoneer was a success from the start.

In 1963, the company was renamed the Kaiser Jeep Corporation and the Willys name disappeared from the automobile industry. The vehicles, however, continued to be manufactured in the old Willys plants in Toledo, Ohio. Kaiser kept the jeep line for seventeen years until 1970.

Advertising for the jeep continued also. One of the most successful campaigns was the one

The Great Escape

Comin' at you—the famous Jeep, CJ-5, the ultimate get-up-an'-go machine. Get a hold of one of these babies, like this sporty Jeep Renegade and you're in for the ride of your life.

She was born to run free far from the pavement. Built to take hard knocks in her stride, the Renegade boasts a brawny suspension, heavy duty axles and a tight 32.9 ft. turning diameter. Roll bar, fender lip extensions and special aluminum wheels come with this spirited beauty. Plus 304 V-8 engine, improved brakes and a dazzling assortment of colors and options.

'74 Jeep Renegade for a really great escape.

Jeep ◢◣ CJ-5
From A Subsidiary of
American Motors Corporation

The first Renegade (1970) was a CJ-5 with the striping, roll bar, and style that attracted many. Gasoline was still inexpensive and the idea of a jeep as a weekend plaything appealed to thousands. The Jeep Corporation sold some 14,000 units at an average price of $2,400.

New Cherokee

It's a Jeep and-a-half

The newest Jeep, vehicle has arrived. Jeep Cherokee. Heir to a tradition of quality and rough road dependability, Cherokee takes up where Jeep CJ-5 leaves off. Youthful and sporty, with the extra room that lets you pack along what you used to leave behind.

Cherokee really stands out where the pavement ends because the famous Jeep 4-wheel drive was specifically designed into Cherokee—most of the competition are merely converted two-wheelers. With greater ground clearance and a higher load capacity than any other sports utility vehicle in its weight class, new Cherokee makes a big difference in the boondocks.

Jeep Cherokee combines this rugged performance with sporty good looks—plus exciting options like Quadra-Trac," Jeep's automatic 4-wheel drive, automatic transmission, power steering, air conditioning and power front disc brakes.

New Jeep Cherokee is the get-away machine your family has been waiting for. It's a Jeep-and-a-half.

Jeep ▮ Cherokee
From A Subsidiary of
American Motors Corporation

SUPER JEEP

Not a bird. Not a plane. But a new thrill under the sun—4-wheel drive fun-mobiling.

At first glance, that same familiar profile, but underneath that super-stripe stands a baby brute with the guts to go where others fear to tread.

Super Jeep® is *all* guts from the brawny suspension to the heavy-duty axle—an open-end design that can turn in just 32.9 ft. And while you're checking out the special color treatment on

the front and rear seats, the roll bar's saying "go!" and the 258 six answers "r-r-i-i-ght!"

Oversize L78 x 15 Polyglas® white wall tires are included along with those black rubber lip extensions on the fenders. Plus chrome front bumper and a safety rail for your more easily flustered passengers. She's available in all kinds of color combinations and lots of extra goodies.

So don't just sit there, hit the trail in a gen-u-ine Super Jeep.

▮ Jeep

Toughest 4-letter word on wheels.

Cherokee was a 2-door sporty wagon for growing young families. Introductory ads presented the vehicle as a "jeep-and-a-half," with lots of load space and rugged good looks. In its introductory year, 1972, 12,000 units were sold at an average retail price of $3,600. The wide-wheel Cherokee Chief, with bold striping and oversize tires, turned the family Cherokee into a dirt-road-race contender.

The Super Jeep (1973). Created because of the temporary unavailability of Renegade wheels, this special package was offered to the public as one-time supersporty jeep. A roll bar, high-visibility hood, and side striping distinguished the Super Jeep from the herd.

launched in 1964 when Kaiser sponsored the "CBS Evening News" with Walter Cronkite. With the Cronkite image behind the jeep, sales soared.

Then, in 1965, the Model CJ-5A was introduced. This marked the first major attempt of the Kaiser Corporation to market the short-wheelbase jeep vehicle to the general public. The advertising agency was Compton of New York City, which succeeded Norman Craig and Kummel as agency of record.

The most popular of the early

Compton campaigns was probably the Jeepster converitble series launched in 1967 with the theme, "Holy Toledo, what a car!" It featured Danny Thomas, the well-known actor and comedian from Toledo, Ohio. However, the most successful of Compton's early campaigns were the 1969 ads for the Wagoneer that presented "The first really new family wagon in years."

In 1970, Roy Chapin, Jr., of the American Motors Corporation made the decision to purchase the entire jeep operation from Kaiser. They

fittingly named it the Jeep Corporation. In this period, the military continued to order the M-151 jeep and the new American Motors Corporation became a major supplier of this new 1/4-ton general-purpose vehicle.

The seventies saw a prolific expansion of jeep vehicles being marketed to the American consumer. Interest in ecology was widening and America's wilderness and back roads were beginning to be explored for recreation. The brand-new sport of 4-wheeling was being enthusias-

A very sporty pickup, the Jeep Honcho was very "macho" too, as its advertising stressed. The Honcho sold 12,000 in its initial year, 1976.

To commemorate twenty-five years of virtually unchanged design, the silver-anniversary CJ-5 was offered in limited numbers in 1978. Only 3,000 units were produced and all were sold in the first week that the ad was run.

tically pursued. A new model, the CJ-5 Universal, was introduced in 1970. The changes were small but important. Windshield wipers moved to the bottom of the windshield; the fuel tank was mounted in the rear; side marker lights appeared; and the introduction of a V-8 304cc engine made this the most formidable CJ ever built. The first Renegade was introduced in the same year and offered a roll bar, swing-away tire carrier, and racing stripe; General George Patton would have liked it. A new

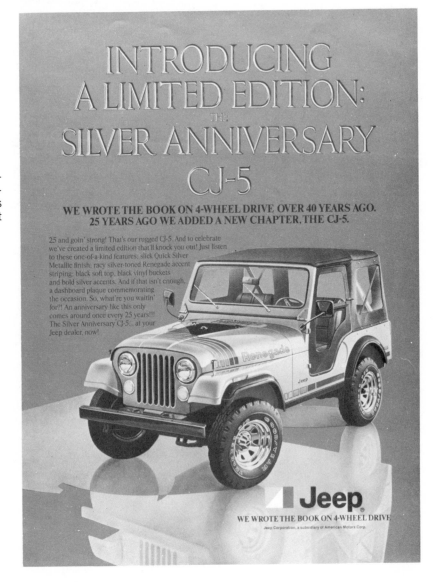

The 1981 Scrambler, a jeep CJ minipickup, is depicted in a fun-inspiring, highly visual print ad. The new vehicle had high appeal for those considering foreign competitors. The Scrambler exceeded all sales expectations.

The simple profile of classic design was never more poignantly portrayed than in the illustration of a brown Laredo in the 1981 "Legendary Jeep" print campaign.

Wagoneer was designed and two new pickup trucks, the J-10 and the heavy-duty J-20; all were introduced in the ambitious campaign for the 1970 models.

In 1972 a 2-door family wagon, the Cherokee, was introduced. Its advertising theme was: "Cherokee, it's a jeep-and-a-half!" Cherokee's successful competition with Blazer and Bronco prompted the introduction of the wide-wheel "muscle" version of the Cherokee, the Cherokee Chief.

In the 1973 model year the proper wheels for the Renegade package were unavailable, so Jeep created a one-time, special-edition CJ, the Super Jeep. It featured chrome bumpers, a roll bar, and an extravagant striping pattern running from head to tailgate.

In the early seventies the theme "Jeep: toughest four-letter word on wheels" was used in advertising and promotion for the entire line. During this time Quadra-Trac, the innovative automatic 4-wheel-drive system developed for Jeep by Borg-Warner, became available on all jeep vehicles. The system, which put an end to the need to get out and lock the hubs, was previously available on the Wagoneer only. And finally, the Jeep Commando, grandson of the venerable Jeepster, was discontinued.

The years that followed saw many more innovative jeep introductions. The 1976 model CJ-7 was designed with a long enough wheelbase to permit an automatic transmission and such "civilized" options as a hardtop and roll-up windows. It was followed by the Jeep Wagoneer Limited, a luxury 4-wheel-drive style, and the very macho Honcho pickup truck, a response to America's turn toward "truckin'."

For the 1978 model year, two new special CJ packages were offered. The Golden Eagle came in dark brown only and had a roll bar, gold-colored wheels, and an angry bird spreadeagled on the hood. And a special limited-edition silver-anniversary jeep commemorated the twenty-five successful years of the modern CJ-5.

In the next model year the Laredo made its debut. All black with a chrome grille and chrome wheels, it replaced the Golden Eagle CJ package which now became available exclusively on the Cherokee.

During the period of the mid-1970s through the early 1980s, the phrase "Jeep wrote the book on 4-wheel drive" was the corporate advertising theme.

The most recent jeep vehicle is the Scrambler, a CJ version of the minipickup. This vehicle was created in direct response to the success of the foreign-made minipickups and to some ingenious Jeep owners who modified their CJs into a small pickup configuration.

Far left: An ad for the American Motors Eagle, a passenger car designed to switch easily from 2-wheel to 4-wheel drive, depicts its remarkable traction in snow. The Eagle represents a major technological innovation as American Motors begins to bridge the gap between 2- and 4-wheel-drive vehicles.

Left: The American Motors Eagle in the 4-door stationwagon configuration has the same remarkable capability of switching while in motion from conventional rear-wheel to full 4-wheel drive.

Left: The high-mobility, multipurpose wheeled vehicle commonly known as the Hummer is the proposed successor to the army's 1/4-ton jeep. Versatility is the key to this vehicle; it will act as reconnaissance, fire support, communications, command and control, and ambulance.

The Jeep in Other Ads

When the name of the game is the unexpected, you'll know what to expect from Safari A-T tires. A sturdy, flexible body for strength and resistance to uncharted surprises. And wide, rugged tread for all-weather, all-terrain traction you can count on. See the complete line — 4-wheel drive, RV and light truck tires — at your Kelly-Springfield dealer. And go on Safari.

Kelly Tires
We're out to change America's tires.

HOW to Fly 3500 Lbs. of Steel without wings...

and Love it when you touch down!

Tom Malloy knows how to build a CJ-5 that thinks it's a "ROCKET", and is! He also knows that his "Rocket" must have the ultimate in suspension or he's got nothing more than a 3500 Lb. nightmare. What shock system holds it all together so Tom's "Rocket" can fly? MICKEY THOMPSON SHOCKS...the ultimate performer designed and manufactured by winners for winners, like Tom Malloy!

AND NOW, from Mickey Thompson Products, Inc., complete "winning" suspension systems...Suspension Kits...Double Shock Kits...Body Lift Kits...Front & Rear Axle Truss Kits...AMC-Eagle Shock Kits...1980 One-Ton Chevy Lift Kits...Heavy-Duty Coil Lift Kits for most applications including 1980 Ford Bronco & F-150 with independent suspension, great for use with WINCHES and SNOW PLOWS. We've got the suspension WINNERS for Standard and Mini-Trucks. BUILT BY WINNERS FOR WINNERS, LIKE YOU!

Visit our booth at the Anaheim SCORE show on March 8 & 9, 1980 — spaces 433 & 434. Dealer inquiries invited. Send $1.00 for your 4-color catalog.

1970 PLACENTIA AVE. COSTA MESA, CALIF. 92627
(714) 645-3118

MICKEY THOMPSON PRODUCTS, Inc.

Photo by Dennis Adler, FOUR WHEELER Magazine

WHEN THE HEAT'S ON, OUR SAND MAN IS ON THE WAY.

When you've got a problem that's too hot to handle, or simply need routine parts and servicing, Cameron always rises to the occasion. Because wherever Cameron equipment is used, we have a field service oasis nearby. Part of the industry's leading worldwide sales, service and warehouse network, with over 85 international locations. Strategically positioned to serve you on land or at sea, 24 hours a day.

We'll get there with the men and machinery you need, when you need them. Men who know the equipment. How to solve your problems. And how important it is to help keep your downtime down.

So, count on Cameron when you need us. Our track record shows we come through.

Cameron OIL TOOLS

CAMERON, WHERE ONE GOOD THING ALWAYS LEADS TO ANOTHER.

Circle 67 on Reader Service Card

126

128

"I won my white water trip by making waves."

"Here I am, Mrs. Herbert's daughter Jennifer, about to kayak downriver . . . in search of 'wild water haystacks'.

"It takes nerve to do that—and it took nerve for me to get here.

"For a crucial new product launch, I actually fought my *boss* for a month. Made waves to keep The Digest as basic.

"I just *knew* he was going on hunches and his own personal feelings. But, when you looked at it professionally, The Digest had what we needed.

"The numbers: 18 million families.

"The long reading time. We had a brand new story to tell . . . with lots of details.

"The credibility: More than any other magazine—certainly more than television. If the product was going to take off, people *had* to believe it would perform just as we said.

"Well, you can see the happy ending. When we exceeded our share point goal, the company gave our whole team a bonus (including my boss). That's when I got my nerve up—and headed for the river."

Reader's Digest

To the Professional, it's the real world.

129

Appendix A

THE U.S. POSTAL SERVICE JEEP

For a machine that suffered the indignity of having been designed and built to replace the army horse, the famed jeep of World War II has come a long way.

Invariably, when one thinks of the squat, squared-off little vehicle, the thought is drenched in olive green, or in an abstract of dull, unobtrusive colors that served to camouflage the tough little friend of every GI from Normandy to Vietnam. Nevertheless, when one thinks of that 1/4-ton vehicle, the picture generally is military. The tough little veteran of World War II, Korea, and Vietnam most likely will be remembered for its combat record—for plodding through the treacherous muds of Italy, for skimming along the wind-blown sands of Africa, for ploughing through the unrelenting snows of Germany and Korea, and for charging through the heat-scorched jungles of the South Pacific and Vietnam. After more than forty years of service in every corner of the world and under every conceivable challenge, the jeep remains today an integral part of the army's military system.

What is not so well recognized, perhaps, is the fact that the battle-tested hero on wheels is now playing—and has played for several years—a significant role in serving Americans in a way that is so taken for granted that it is almost overlooked.

In this peacetime role, the jeep has changed its colors. It has shed its drab combat paint for red, white, and blue. Its mission: delivering the mails for the U.S. Postal Service.

This peacetime version of what certainly has become a legend has gained quite a reputation on its own. And it has proved so efficient and so effective a vehicle for the U.S. Postal Service that in 1981, they placed an order for 18,000 more vehicles and announced plans to purchase another 30,000 over the next few years from the AM General Corporation, which manufactures the versatile vehicle.

Known officially as the DJ-5 Dispatcher, the postal jeep is a familiar sight in the cities and on the farms, where it delivers the nation's letters, packages, Christmas cards, junk mail, and all the other mailed greetings in rain, snow, heat, or "gloom of night." It serves as an important delivery vehicle in the fleet of postal vehicles, and if one listens to the men who maintain that fleet, the jeep has proved to be one of the best friends the letter carrier ever had.

"In my personal opinion," said Cullen Dunning, acting general manager of vehicle services at Postal Service headquarters in Washington, D.C., "the Jeep is the best vehicle we've ever had for delivering mail. It's small. It's compact. It's maneuverable. And it's economical to operate. At least, it's as economical as you can get with all the stop-and-go driving that we do."

There are, of course, some major differences between the postal jeep and the military jeep. The military jeep has 4-wheel drive, while the postal jeep only has 2-wheel drive. The suspension systems differ. The postal jeep has right-hand drive and a crazy-looking large mirror poking out the side to give the letter carrier a better—and safer—view.

"If we have a problem with it," Dunning said, "we just are not aware of it. Considering the number of the vehicles we have in our fleet, it's been extremely safe, too."

Tom Martin, the vehicle manager for the Postal Service is San Bruno, California, supports that contention. "We really do not look upon the jeep as a safety problem at all," he explained. "You've got to recognize that it has a short wheelbase when you drive it. And that's the key—how the vehicle is driven. Our

DJ-5L DISPATCHER 100
1/4-TON TRUCK, 4X2

AM General Corporation

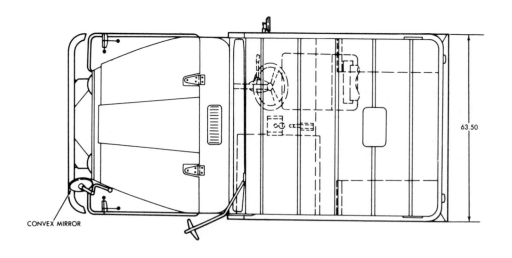

CONVEX MIRROR

63.50

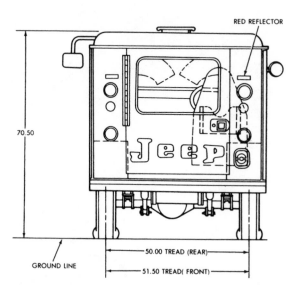

RED REFLECTOR

70.50

GROUND LINE

50.00 TREAD (REAR)

51.50 TREAD(FRONT)

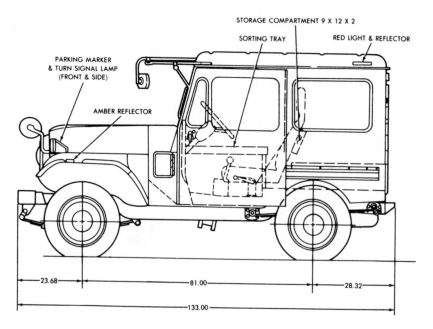

STORAGE COMPARTMENT 9 X 12 X 2

SORTING TRAY

RED LIGHT & REFLECTOR

PARKING MARKER
& TURN SIGNAL LAMP
(FRONT & SIDE)

AMBER REFLECTOR

23.68

81.00

28.32

133.00

VEHICLE SHOWN WITH OPTIONAL RIGHT-HAND DRIVE.

132

The jeep with the most mileage: This eight-year-old jeep at North Wildwood, New Jersey, has seen 50,000 miles of use and is ready for resale. The letter carrier who delivered the mail with it during those eight years stands alongside the vehicle.

The U.S. postal jeep as it is first seen off the assembly line.

drivers, I think, are well trained in handling all the vehicles they drive. As a result, we don't have any more accidents with that type of vehicle than we do with any other."

The Postal Service has approximately 90,000 DJ-5s in its inventory from coast to coast, including approximately 350 electrically operated jeeps that are being used primarily on the West Coast on a test basis. The routes are relatively short and level in the Los Angeles and San Bernadino areas where the tests are going on. Because these jeeps are battery powered, they help reduce pollution in that smog-ridden region.

The vehicles are powered by 27-cell batteries, generating 54 volts. They are driven five hours a day and then recharged overnight. At a cruising speed of 30 miles an hour, the battery-powered vehicles have a range of approximately 20 miles, with some 250 stops and starts between charges.

The electric jeeps were first put into use in 1971, according to Robert K. St. Francis at Postal Service headquarters. St. Francis, director of the Office of Fleet Management, points out that additional battery-powered vehicles are now being introduced and will be used over a wider geographical area, including Florida, Texas, and some states along the East Coast.

"We still have a long way to go technologically with these battery-powered vehicles," he emphasizes. "Basically, we still are in the experimentation stage, and we will have to see some breakthroughs in battery technology and other areas before we could suggest wider use of those vehicles."

The use of the jeep for delivering the mail began in 1968. At that time, postal officials looked at their 3-wheeled delivery vehicle then in use and decided they needed something faster, larger, and more stable. Faced with the ever-increasing volume of mail and the problems with faster traffic conditions, they sought a more reliable vehicle, but one with low maintenance costs, good handling, and above-average performance. As they looked around, they were impressed with the jeep. As a result, they prepared specifications for 24,000 4-cylinder vehicles to be purchased by the government's General Services Administration, subject to competitive procurement procedures.

Notwithstanding the fact that the Postal Service called for numerous modifications to meet its own unique requirements, existing and proved technology and experience could be utilized, and thus the AM General Corporation in Detroit—the

world's largest producer of tactical wheeled vehicles, including the jeep—was the low and successful bidder.

AM General's experience with jeeps, of course, went back to World War II. And because that company was able to make use of its experience and technology, postal officials estimate savings of from $3 million to $5 million on the first order of DJ-5s. In subsequent years, the Postal Service has continued to buy the DJ, again through competitive procurement. Those purchases included 16,000 vehicles in 1970/71, 21,000 in 1973/74, 13,000 in 1975/76, 6,000 in 1977, and 9,000 in 1978/79.

Through the years, there have been many changes to meet the needs of the Postal Service. City routes, rural deliveries, tropical as well as frigid climates, flat terrain and mountain roads—all must be served under stop-and-go conditions. For this, the conventional commercial vehicle (and the Postal Service has tried them) has not proved to be as reliable as the functionally designed jeep, postal officials explain.

In addition, the letter carriers prefer the specially designed vehicle over the regular commercial one. They maintain that the jeep, because of its right-hand drive, is safer than the conventional vehicle. It also is easier to handle. It carries more mail and carries it in a manner that makes delivery more productive. They argue, too, that the jeep has proved itself much more reliable and sturdy than the old vans that they replaced.

For vehicles currently in use, the Postal Service has its DJs on a 5,000-mile, twice-a-year maintenance cycle. Vehicles that generate more than 5,000 miles per annum

are scheduled for additional maintenance. The maintenance work is done either in the Postal Service's own shops or under contract with local dealers and garages.

The vehicles undergo testing at the American Motors Corporation plant in South Bend, Indiana, and at the Postal Service's own research and development facilities in Rockville, Maryland. In addition, feedback reports from the letter carriers are encouraged to keep the fleet in topflight condition.

Even after years of faithful mail service, the postal jeeps are proving to be what must be one of the government's best buys, a fact that has gone unnoticed by the public as a general rule. The Postal Service's experience with the resale of the vehicles has been nothing short of remarkable—excellent no matter in what part of the country they are offered for sale.

One of the most successful resale programs has been that in Memphis, Tennessee. Charles Kainer, branch manager for vehicle services with the Postal Service there, is averaging a 75 to 80 percent return on investment with the DJs, and sometimes the return is as high as 95 percent. In one sale, he was able to get $1,900 for a vehicle the Postal Service had paid $2,047 for eight years earlier.

In 1980, 2,705 vehicles were sold out of the Memphis office. The average rate of return on all vehicles, Kainer says, was 65 percent. But the return on the DJs averaged much higher than the others.

The Postal Service is allowed to spend $115 per vehicle to refurbish it for resale, Kainer explained. Much of that is taken up by the repainting, which must be done to wipe out the Postal Service recognition. Generally, however, the vehicles are cleaned up and placed in good operating condition, too.

"We make no guarantees," said Kainer, although he admits that the customers have come to expect good service from the vehicles. "If we know of a defect, we'll tell them about it. And the customer has seven days to return the vehicle if he or she finds something drastically wrong with it."

Some of the vehicles are bought by individuals, some by businesses, and some by dealers. Some even go overseas. The only people excluded from buying are Postal Service employees. Many of the used jeeps are purchased by construction firms and by companies that make deliveries, such as laundries and food markets.

"Having proved itself as a good delivery vehicle," said Kainer, "the jeep offers many businesses a vehicle of excellent productivity with little cost." The customers are thrilled with the vehicles, he continued. "We hardly ever have any complaints, and I have people coming back for more all the time. They'll call and ask to be informed when more are going to be offered for sale."

Thus, the little vehicle that gained fame on the battlefield is proving to be a highly useful spinoff. The jeep not only provides a useful service in fulfilling its assigned mission. It also proves a good investment for the American taxpayer.

That's not bad for something that started out just to replace the horse.

Appendix B

THE MANY FACES OF THE Jeep

The Bantam Model BRC (Bantam Reconnaissance Car). Approximately 2,500 units were produced and lend-leased to England and Russia.

The first real jeep, the Willys "Quad." It was the pilot model in the competition between Ford, Bantam, and Willys.

The Ford GP "Pygmy." This model was powered by a Ford tractor engine.

The single most distinguishing feature of the jeep vehicle has been its characteristic vertical slotted grille. Over the years, this grille has changed and evolved—sometimes subtly, often drastically. The following views illustrate those variations. It is important to notice that even through considerable evolution, the jeep grille has always maintained its optimistic, "toothy" grin.

The Willys MA. This vehicle was the result of the "crash diet" Willys engineers imposed on the vehicle in order to get their entry down to government-specified weight.

The final configuration of the Willys MB, with the familiar 9-slot grille face that has been synonymous with the name Jeep. This design remained standard from 1942 to 1945 with only slight modification.

An early Willys MB. This slatted grille design was the final victor in the competition to produce the military 4 × 4 requirements.

The CJ-2A, the first civilian jeep with sealed-beam headlights and directional signals where the blackout lights had been. This version had a seven-slotted grille.

The CJ-3B. A slightly raised hood that housed the new, larger F-head Hurricane engine characterized the front face of the CJ-3B.

The Jeepster—a rather remarkable change of face but still wholly compatible with the classic jeep image. The Jeepster grille was toothy and formed a slightly forward V which was chrome-plated, a luxury that war-weary Americans found appealing.

The DJ-5, a 2-wheel-drive jeep-type vehicle dubbed the Dispatcher. It is used for light-duty courier service, most prominently by the U.S. Postal Service in mail delivery. The DJ-5 is characterized by its 5-slot grille.

The CJ-5—also identical to the M-38A1. The fenders and hood were curved to add aesthetics and streamlining. This face, first introduced in 1951 during the Korean Conflict, is nearly identical to the vehicles that are being produced today.

The Jeepster Commando, upgraded with a new front grille but very much within the jeep family image. The primary difference is a broad, sweeping hood that encompasses nearly the entire front of the vehicle.

The M-151—the military 1/4-ton 4 × 4 M-151. The successor to the model M-38A1, it was designed by Ford and saw action in Vietnam. The characteristic vertical grille was changed to horizontal but was still essentially jeeplike in its overall impression.

The CJ-10—a vehicle not yet in production but proposed for the early 1980s. Its CJ cab rests on a J-10 truck body. The headlights and signal lamps have been moved to the fenders, and the grille has 13 slots for ample airflow to the engine.

The CJ-5 as it looks today. The rounded top of the windshield has been squared off and the windshield wipers operate from below the glass. The fender extensions are compatible with the larger wheel and all-terrain tire.

The "Hummer," the American Motors entry for the new army contract. The totally redesigned vehicle happily sports the traditional slotted grille.

140

Picture Credits

Index